THE BOSTON CELTICS

An Illustrated Timeline

BY GARY WASHBURN

REEDY PRESS

Reedy Press
PO Box 5131
St. Louis, MO 63139, USA
www.reedypress.com

Library of Congress Control Number: 2024939321

ISBN: 9781681064444

Cover and interior design by Eric Marquard

Front cover images courtesy of Getty Images. L to R: Andrew. D Bernstein (and court image), Dick Raphael, Nathaniel S. Butler, Jared Wickerham, Focus On Sport

Back cover image courtesy of Getty Images pool photographer.

All interior photos courtesy of Getty Images unless otherwise noted.

Printed in the United States of America
25 26 27 28 5 4 3 2

THE BOSTON CELTICS

An Illustrated Timeline

BY GARY WASHBURN

Bill Russell looks at the camera during a time-out in the waning moments of Game 4 in the 1967 Eastern Conference Finals against the 76ers at the Boston Garden.
COURTESY OF GETTY IMAGES

Contents

Acknowledgments

THERE ARE MANY PEOPLE I would like to thank for their support in writing this book. The first is my wife, Annya, who has embraced my love for journalism in a way that I couldn't imagine. I could not have completed this without her. My mother, Robin, has always been in my corner and encouraged my growth and education. My late father, Michael, gave me my love of sports. I hope he is proud. Thank you to the sports editors who took an interest in my success, including Ron Matthews and Joe Sullivan, as well as the great Eric Sondheimer for teaching me the basics as a young reporter and helping mold my career. Thanks also to those folks at the *Boston Globe* who have encouraged and supported me.

There are numerous colleagues and friends who have been through this journey with me: James Black, Sherrod Blakely, Rod Boone, Trevor Borden, Jerry Brewer, Corey Brown, Howard Bryant, Dan Connolly, Sekou Dilday, Vincent Goodwill, Chris Haynes, Telly Hughes, Greg Lee, Alex Lewis, Kwani Lunis, Kevin Redd, Jarrod Rudolph, Chris Scott, Marc Smith, Marc Spears, Harry Taylor, Keith Taylor, Marcus Thompson, Edward Wilkins, Francis Williams, Keith Pompey, and Jabari Young. My stepfather Jimmy Manor, my brothers Britton and Brandon Washburn. And the public relations staff for the Celtics, including Jeff Twiss, Christian Megliola, Taylor Kielpinski-Rogers, and Brian Olive.

And to those who have read my stories and coverage of the Celtics over the years, thank you for your feedback and hopefully you will enjoy all the moments of this book. It's been an amazing experience covering the Celtics and the NBA during these dozen-plus years. And thank you to those folks I worked with at MLB.com, *Long Beach Press-Telegram*, *Los Angeles Daily News*, *Contra Costa Times*, and the *Seattle Post-Intelligencer*.

Larry Bird (left) and Danny Ainge battle for position against the Detroit Pistons at the Boston Garden in 1986.
COURTESY OF GETTY IMAGES

Introduction

THE BOSTON CELTICS are one of the most prestigious franchises in the history of American sports. They have won 18 championships, the most of any team in the history of the NBA and one more than their rival Minneapolis/Los Angeles Lakers.

The tradition of the organization is rich, with all-time greats such as Bill Russell, Bob Cousy, Sam Jones, John Havlicek, Dave Cowens, Larry Bird, Kevin McHale, Robert Parish, Jo Jo White, Kevin Garnett, Ray Allen, and Paul Pierce all winning championships in Celtics green.

The franchise has risen, resurrected, and risen again four separate times, becoming the model NBA organization with championships in the 1950s and '60s with the great combination of Russell and Cousy, and then returning to prominence in the 1970s under Cowens, Havlicek, and White.

General manager and president Red Auerbach, who was the mastermind behind nine of those championships as a coach, made the brilliant move of drafting a forward from Indiana State University named Larry Bird a year before his college eligibility expired. Bird changed the course of franchise history, leading the Celtics to three championships and winning three consecutive MVP awards.

The Celtics have experienced their share of hard times. The post-Bird era was difficult, and the franchise tragically lost first-round pick Len Bias and budding superstar Reggie Lewis within seven years. The organization suffered with losing seasons, ineffective coaches, and failed roster decisions.

The drafting of Kansas forward Paul Pierce in 1998 was a sign of return to respectability, and when Auerbach hired former player Danny Ainge to run the front office and Ainge hired Doc Rivers as coach, the Celtics rose again. Ainge made two franchise-altering trades in 2007 when he acquired All-Stars Kevin Garnett and Ray Allen to join Pierce.

That trio would lift the Celtics to their first championship in 22 years. And after another 16 years, this new generation of Celtics stars such as Jayson Tatum, Jaylen Brown, Al Horford, Derrick White, and Jrue Holiday helped Boston to return to the mountain top with a championship in 2024, cementing the Celtics as the model franchise in professional sports.

This book is an artistic and visual view of that journey to prosperity, a look at the history of this organization, the championships, the players, the amazing moments, the unforgettable times, the difficult years.

The collection of 175 moments serves as a photo biography of the Boston Celtics, from Walter Brown to Jayson Tatum, from Bob Cousy to Rajon Rondo, from K.C. Jones to Marcus Smart, from Charlie Scott to Kevin Garnett. Of course, it was difficult to pick only 175 moments in the rich 78-year history of the Celtics, dating back to when they entered the Basketball Association of America with visionary owner Walter Brown, but we selected moments from all of those glorious eras that will conjure flashbacks for fans of all ages.

We hope you enjoy the memories, learn more about the history of the Celtics organization, and appreciate the amazing photos and recollections that allow you to reminisce about the past while also looking forward to the Celtics' bright future.

The Boston Celtics pose for a team portrait circa 1948 in Boston.
COURTESY OF GETTY IMAGES

The Beginning of the Celtics Franchise

THE BOSTON CELTICS were born on June 6, 1946, as Walter Brown, manager of the Boston Garden, took a mortgage out on his home and helped form the Basketball Association of America (BAA), with the Celtics as one of the original teams. Prior to the NBA, the BAA was one of three major American basketball leagues and began with 11 teams, including the Philadelphia Warriors, New York Knickerbockers, Toronto Huskies, Providence Steamrollers, Chicago Stags, St. Louis Bombers, Cleveland Rebels, Detroit Falcons, Washington Capitols, and Pittsburgh Ironmen. The Celtics' first draft pick was guard Eddie "Bulbs" Ehlers out of Purdue, who was taken third overall in 1947. The Celtics' first coach was John "Honey" Russell, a fascinating man who played professional basketball for 25 years and also coached at Seton Hall and Manhattan College during that span before taking the Celtics job in 1946. He coached Boston for two seasons, leading the Celtics to the playoffs in his second year before returning to college coaching. The Celtics played three years in the BAA before agreeing to join the National Basketball Association (NBA) on August 3, 1949. Ten BAA teams and seven National Basketball League teams merged to form the NBA. The Celtics would play their home games at Boston Garden, sharing the arena with the NHL's Bruins.

The Great Walter Brown

THE MAN WHO started the Celtics franchise, Walter Brown, was the team's first owner and helped conceive the BAA, the league that eventually merged with the NBA. Brown mortgaged his home to purchase the rights to the Celtics and then aided the club in joining the NBA. The Celtics won seven championships for Brown before his untimely death in 1964, and the NBA responded by naming its championship trophy after Brown. He was also instrumental in the development of ice hockey in the United States, is a member of the Hockey Hall of Fame, and was the owner of the NHL's Bruins from 1951 until 1964. The Celtics retired No. 1 in honor of Brown on October 17, 1964, a month after his passing. The Walter Brown Arena hosted the Boston University men's hockey team for several years. Brown was succeeded in Celtics ownership by Lou Pieri, who was a co-owner with Brown's widow Marjorie.

Celtics owner Walter Brown poses for a picture circa 1950 in Boston.
COURTESY OF GETTY IMAGES

Celtics Draft the NBA's First Black Player, Chuck Cooper

ON APRIL 25, 1950, The Celtics broke the color line in the NBA, drafting the league's first Black player in Chuck Cooper, a bruising forward out of Duquesne University. The NBA was in its beginning stages when Cooper was drafted, and the Celtics didn't hesitate to integrate the league. Team owner Walter Brown told reporters he did not care what color Cooper was, and that the Celtics were drafting him. He was picked in the second round, 13th overall. Earl Lloyd and Nat "Sweetwater" Clifton were also signed by NBA teams prior to the 1950 season, with Lloyd the first to make his debut on October 31, 1950. Cooper played four seasons with the Celtics, averaging 6.8 points and 6.6 rebounds in 272 games. He then was traded to the Milwaukee Hawks and finished his career with the Fort Wayne Pistons. He also continued to break barriers after his basketball career, becoming Pittsburgh's first Black head of parks and recreation. Cooper's No. 15 was retired by Duquesne, and he was inducted into the Naismith Memorial Basketball Hall of Fame in 2019 as a player. The Celtics would not only draft the first Black player but also field the first Black starting five in 1964 and then name the first Black head coach, Bill Russell, in 1966.

The Celtics' Chuck Cooper jumping up to catch the basketball.
COURTESY OF GETTY IMAGES

Ed Macauley #22 and Bob Cousy #14 pose with Celtics' owner Walter Brown in 1951.
COURTESY OF GETTY IMAGES

The Celtics Host the 1951 All-Star Game

IN THE NBA'S second season, Boston Garden hosted the league's first All-Star Game, matching up the East and West teams on March 2, 1951. Celtics owner Walter Brown devised the idea of an exhibition game between the NBA's two divisions as a way to divert attention away from the college basketball point-shaving scandal. Brown offered the Boston Garden as the venue and also agreed to pay the cost of the game. The East team had 10 players and was represented by two Celtics—Ed Macauley and Bob Cousy. The West team included such players as George Mikan and Vern Mikkelsen of the Minneapolis Lakers. Dolph Schayes of the Syracuse Nationals and Joe Fulks and Paul Arizin of the Philadelphia Warriors were also on the East team. The East team took control early and cruised to a 111–94 win over the West. Macauley was named the first-ever All-Star MVP with 20 points and six rebounds, while Cousy added eight points and eight assists playing in front of the home fans. The game attendance was 10,094, nearly three times the league average attendance. The NBA then would make the All-Star Game a yearly staple, and Boston would host the game in four of the game's first 14 years.

The Trade for Bill Russell

BILL RUSSELL WAS not drafted by the Boston Celtics. That's a long-running myth. Russell was actually drafted second overall by the St. Louis Hawks in 1956 after winning consecutive NCAA titles at the University of San Francisco. But Russell would never play a game for the Hawks. Celtics president Red Auerbach figured his team needed a young, talented defender and big man to lead his franchise to the next level. But acquiring such a talent would come at a cost. The Celtics knew they would have to offer the Hawks one of their top players to consummate the deal. Boston offered future Hall of Famer "Easy" Ed Macauley, who had averaged nearly 19 points in his six years with the Celtics, and another Hall of Famer, draft pick Cliff Hagan, for the rights to Russell. The Rochester Royals actually owned the first pick of the 1956 draft but felt they could not afford Russell, thus making him available to the Hawks. Macauley was a St. Louis native and wanted to go home, making the trade easier to facilitate. In Russell, the Celtics received a player who would become one of the most impactful in the history of professional sports. He won 11 championships for the Celtics, including two as a player-coach, and became the centerpiece of the NBA's greatest dynasty. Russell was a 12-time All-Star in his 13 seasons, was inducted into the Naismith Hall of Fame as a player and coach, and had his No. 6 retired by the Celtics in 1972.

The University of San Francisco's Bill Russell plays in a game against Loyola of Los Angeles on February 4, 1955.
COURTESY OF GETTY IMAGES

Frank Ramsey, the NBA's First Sixth Man

ONE OF THE more overlooked players in Celtics history, Frank Ramsey was one of the NBA's ultimate winners, earning seven championships in his nine seasons, preceding the likes of John Havlicek and Kevin McHale as the Celtics' sixth man. Boston drafted the guard-forward with the sixth overall pick in 1953 out of the University of Kentucky, and he became a reliable scorer and rebounder both off the bench and in the starting lineup. Coach Red Auerbach helped create the sixth man role by using Ramsey off the bench but playing starter's minutes. He flourished against the second units of opposing teams. Ramsey immediately helped the Celtics in 1954–55, averaging 11.2 points. He missed his second season to serve in the US Army, and when he returned in January 1957 he immediately returned to help the Celtics to their first NBA championship, scoring 16 points in the deciding Game 7 against the St. Louis Hawks. Ramsey averaged double figures in eight of his nine seasons and finished in the NBA's top 20 scoring in three seasons. He was considered reliable and filled his complementary role perfectly, a staple of those late 1950s and early 1960s title teams. The Celtics showed their appreciation by retiring his No. 23 on October 16, 1965, and Ramsey was inducted into the Naismith Memorial Basketball Hall of Fame in 1982.

Frank Ramsey dribbles for a mock action portrait during the late 1950s.
COURTESY OF GETTY IMAGES

The First Championship: The 1956–57 Celtics

THERE WERE TWO major factors that separated the 1955–56 Celtics from the 1956–57 version: Bill Russell and Tom Heinsohn. The Celtics scored historically big when they acquired the rights to Russell from the St. Louis Hawks and later selected Heinsohn, a local product from Holy Cross, with the sixth overall pick. The Celtics finished the regular season with a 44–28 record, five games better than the previous season. The scoring catalyst was 30-year-old Bill Sharman, who led the team with 21.1 points per game. But it was also the best season of Bob Cousy's career; he was league MVP, averaging 20.6 points and 7.5 assists. Russell led the league in rebounds, and Heinsohn was named Rookie of the Year. The Celtics made quick work of the Syracuse Nationals in the first round of the playoffs, sweeping them in three games. The incomparable Russell averaged 28 rebounds in the series, besting counterpart Dolph Schayes. The Finals were more of a challenge, with the Celtics losing the opening game to rival St. Louis before rallying to force a Game 7. In one of the most epic games in NBA history, the Celtics bested the Hawks 125–123 in double overtime. Russell scored the game-tying basket in regulation and then raced back to block Jack Coleman's layup attempt near the buzzer. Heinsohn led Boston with 37 points, saving the Celtics on a night when Cousy and Sharman were a combined 5-for-40. It was the first of the 18 titles for the franchise.

Members of the Celtics' 1957 NBA Championship team during the ceremony honoring the 50th anniversary.
COURTESY OF GETTY IMAGES

Bob Cousy #14 lunges for a loose ball that the Saint Louis Hawks' Slater Martin (left) has just scooped up. Bill Sharman #21, and the Hawks' Chuck Share (kneeling, right) watch the action.
COURTESY OF GETTY IMAGES

Game 7 of the 1957 Finals

IN A SERIES that featured 10 Naismith Memorial Basketball Hall of Famers, the Celtics, seeking their first NBA championship, faced off with the St. Louis Hawks in an epic series that went to double overtime in Game 7—the second double-overtime game of the series. The first half of Game 7 was tight, with the Hawks holding a 53–51 lead. The Celtics forged ahead in the third quarter, outscoring the Hawks 32–24. As usual, the Celtics had a hard time containing Hall of Famer Bob Pettit, who finished with 39 points and 19 rebounds and led the Hawks' fourth-quarter comeback. The Hawks led by two in the final seconds when rookie Bill Russell scored a layup and then sprinted down the floor to block a layup attempt by Jack Coleman, sending the game into overtime. Bill Sharman had a chance to win the title in the first overtime but his 20-footer caromed off the rim. Jim Loscutoff gave the Celtics a two-point lead on free throws—he scored just 3 points all game, all on free throws. With two seconds left, the Hawks responded by throwing the inbounds pass the length of the court. The ball hit the backboard and landed in the hands of Pettit, who then missed a 15-footer at the buzzer, sending the Boston crowd into a frenzy. The Celtics won behind Tom Heinsohn's 37 points and 23 rebounds, while Russell added 19 points and 32 rebounds. Bob Cousy and Bill Sharman finished a combined 5-for-40 shooting, making the Celtics win even more improbable.

Cousy Wins 1957 MVP

BOB COUSY IS considered by many to be the NBA's first great point guard, the quarterback of those championship teams in the 1950s and early 1960s. But Cousy was much more than a distributor. He was a prolific scorer in a day when scoring was more difficult in the NBA, shooting percentages were lower, and defenses dominated. Cousy's best season may have been 1956–57, when he averaged 20.7 points, 7.5 assists, and 4.8 rebounds in winning his lone Most Valuable Player award, the first Celtic to win the honor. Cousy and Bill Sharman would team up to help Boston to its first NBA championship, and Cousy was named to his seventh All-Star Game. Cousy began the 1956–57 season with a 35-point performance against his hometown team, the New York Knicks, at Madison Square Garden. He matched that total in the Celtics' next visit to the Garden. He also dished out 19 assists along with 21 points in a win over Syracuse. It was a brilliant season for Cousy, one that proved he was much more than an assist man.

Bob Cousy is presented with the Outstanding Player award from NBA President Maurice Podoloff following the NBA All-Star Game at the Boston Garden on January 15, 1957.
COURTESY OF GETTY IMAGES

The Great Bill Sharman

BEFORE BILL RUSSELL the Celtics had Bill Sharman, a brilliant shooting guard who was named to the Naismith Memorial Basketball Hall of Fame and the NBA's all-time 50th and 75th anniversary teams. Sharman, who played at USC, was the second-round pick of the Washington Capitols in 1950. After being taken by the Fort Wayne Pistons in the dispersal draft, Sharman was acquired by the Celtics for center Chuck Share in a shrewd move that would help the team to multiple titles. Sharman spent 10 seasons with the Celtics and played in eight All-Star games. He averaged 18.1 points and led the NBA seven times in free throw percentage. Sharman was also named to the first-team All-NBA squad four times and second team three times. Sharman was also a World War II veteran (which is why he was 24 years old when drafted), and he later became a Hall of Fame coach and NBA executive. Sharman also played baseball in the Brooklyn Dodgers' minor league system. As a coach, Sharman led the rival Los Angeles Lakers to the 1971–72 NBA championship a year after leading the Utah Stars to the ABA title. His No. 21 was retired by the Celtics in 1966.

Bill Sharman takes a bow during the *NBA at 50* presentation in Cleveland, Ohio on February 9, 1997.
COURTESY OF GETTY IMAGES

Red Auerbach Joins the Celtics

AFTER THE 1949–50 season, the Celtics were desperate for a coaching upgrade. Owner Walter Brown decided on Red Auerbach, who had coached the Washington Capitols of the BAA and the Tri-Cities Blackhawks. Before Auerbach joined the Celtics prior to the 1950–51 season, Boston had made just one playoff appearance in the previous four seasons, a first-round elimination in 1948. After taking over in 1950, Auerbach orchestrated the trade for shooting guard Bill Sharman and then drafted the great Bob Cousy, who could not come to an agreement with Tri-Cities, the team that drafted him and then was available when Chicago Stags folded. Auerbach led the Celtics to a second-place finish in the Eastern Division in 1950–51 and a playoff appearance. Seven years after taking over as coach, Auerbach led the Celtics to their first NBA championship behind a crew of future Hall of Famers including Bill Russell, Cousy, Sharman, and Frank Ramsey. Through astute trades and brilliant coaching, Auerbach turned the Celtics into the model NBA franchise. In Auerbach's 16 years a coach, the most successful of any coach in professional sports history, the Celtics won nine championships and lost in the finals of another. He was inducted into the Naismith Memorial Hall of Fame as a coach in 1969 and became president of the organization after his retirement from coaching.

Head coach Red Auerbach lights up a cigar during the 1960 NBA game at the Boston Garden.
COURTESY OF GETTY IMAGES

Coach Red Auerbach (center) and referee Sid Borgia (right) disagree on a point during a Celtics–Warriors game at Boston Garden.
COURTESY OF GETTY IMAGES

The 1958 Setback

AT THE END of the 1957–1958 season, the Celtics appeared poised to go back-to-back for the first time, winning 49 games in the regular season as second-year center Bill Russell won his first MVP award and Boston coasted to a five-game series win over the rival Philadelphia Warriors in the Eastern Division Finals. The NBA Final opponent was a familiar one in the St. Louis Hawks, the only team in the Western Division with a winning record (41–31). The matchup, however, was difficult. The Hawks made a statement by winning Game 1 at Boston Garden behind 33 points from Hall of Famer Cliff Hagan. The teams split the next two games before the Celtics rallied to tie the series at two, but Russell wasn't a part of that Game 4 win. The Celtics big man had suffered a badly sprained ankle and a chip fracture in Game 3 and would not play for the rest of the series. Without a menacing defensive presence in the middle, the Celtics struggled defensively against Hagan and Bob Pettit, who took turns gashing their defense in the final few games. The Celtics were handed a two-point loss in Game 5 at Boston Garden, and then Pettit scored 18 of St. Louis' final 21 points and they edged the Celtics 110–109 to win the title. After the loss, Celtics coach Red Auerbach refused to use Russell's injury as an excuse. He said the Celtics were just beaten by the better team.

Celtics Drop 173 Points on the Minneapolis Lakers, February 27, 1959

HIGH-SCORING GAMES weren't all that common in the early NBA, but 20 years before the introduction of the 3-point shot, the Celtics set a team record for points in a 173–149 regulation win over the Minneapolis Lakers on February 27, 1959. It was a masterful performance by Bob Cousy, who dished out a career-high 28 assists while also scoring 31 points, and Tom Heinsohn, who set a career high with 43 points to go with 11 rebounds. The Celtics shot 50 percent from the field and 78 percent from the free throw line. They scored 90 points in the second half and 52 in the fourth quarter, all without the luxury of a 3-point shot. Seven Celtics scored in double figures, including Bill Sharman with 29 and Frank Ramsey with 20. Even more incredibly, they set this record without help of Bill Russell, who missed the game with an injury. It was one of just two games that Russell missed that season.

Bill Sharman puts on a burst of speed and catches Dick Garmaker of the Minneapolis Lakers flat-footed as he drives in for a layup in a game at the Boston Garden.
COURTESY OF GETTY IMAGES

The 1959 Title Run

THE CELTICS WERE coming off back-to-back NBA title apperances in 1959, and the core of their team—Bill Russell, Sam Jones, and Frank Ramsey—was just entering its prime. The club also added rookie defender K.C. Jones to join veteran stalwarts Bill Sharman and Bob Cousy. The Celtics improved their regular season record by three games with 52 wins and again won the Eastern Division. What changed was the Celtics' road to the championship. The Syracuse Nationals replaced the Philadelphia Warriors as their Eastern Division rival, and the Celtics needed another seven-game series to dispose of a club that included Hall of Famers Dolph Schayes and George Yardley. In a series where each team won alternate games, the Celtics edged the Nationals 130–125 in Game 7. Seven Celtics scored in double figures, including Bill Russell, who scored 18 points to go with with 32 rebounds as Boston pulled away. The NBA Finals were a bit easier, as the Celtics faced off against the Lakers (still in Minneapolis) for the first time. Minneapolis reached the Finals despite a 33–39 record, making the Lakers the first NBA team to play in the championship series with a losing record. Its good fortune ran out against the Celtics, who swept the series in four games. Russell, then becoming one of the most dominant players in the league, averaged 29.5 rebounds in the series, giving the Celtics their second title in three years. Boston was the first NBA team to win the Finals in a sweep.

The Celtics celebrate in the dressing room after beating the Minneapolis Lakers, 118–113, to win the NBA title. The Celtics swept the series.
COURTESY OF GETTY IMAGES

Boston Celtics' Bill Russell #6, hooks a shot during the NBA championship's final game in 1960 against the St. Louis Hawks.
COURTESY OF GETTY IMAGES

The 1960 Title

AGAIN, THE CELTICS were the most dominant team in the NBA, finishing with a 59–16 record as the season increased in length to 75 games from 72 games. It was a familiar cast of characters, with Bill Russell and Bob Cousy along with a still-All-Star-level Bill Sharman and Tom Heinsohn. Heinsohn emerged as the team's leading scoring threat while Russell was second in the league in rebounding at 24 per game. Once again the opponent in the Eastern Division Final was the Philadelphia Warriors, whose sensational rookie center Wilt Chamberlain beat out Russell for the rebounding title. The Celtics raced out to a 3–1 series lead behind the dominance of Russell, who had 26 points and 39 rebounds in Game 3. Chamberlain responded with an astounding 50-point, 35-rebound effort to keep the Warriors alive in Game 5. The Celtics managed to hold Chamberlain to 26 points in Game 6, and Russell led Boston with 25 points and 25 rebounds to close out the series. The St. Louis Hawks again stood between the Celtics and another title, and this series also went to a deciding seventh game. Boston used a 41-point second period to pull away from the Hawks 122–103 in Game 7. Russell finished with a whopping 35 rebounds while Frank Ramsey led the Celtics with 24 points, helping Boston reach its third title in four years and continuing the dynasty.

The 1961 Champs

THE 1961 CELTICS may have been the most dominant of their title teams in the 1960s, needing only five games to dispose of the Syracuse Nationals and St. Louis Hawks in the playoffs after winning 57 regular-season games. Bill Sharman, in what would be his final NBA season, averaged 16 points while Bob Cousy, another of the team's 30-somethings, finished second on the team with 18.1 points. But it was becoming apparent that the cornerstones of the franchise were Tom Heinsohn, who led the club in scoring, and Bill Russell, who was the league's best defender. Russell won the second of his five MVP awards by averaging 16.9 points and 23.9 rebounds. Boston polished off the Nationals in the Eastern Division Finals behind 31 rebounds per game from Russell and 20 points per game from Sharman. The Celtics then exerted their dominance in the Finals against the Hawks, as six players scored in double figures and Russell again commanded the boards. Sharman would finish his career as an eight-time All-Star and four-time champion, and his No. 21 would eventually be retired.

The World Champion Boston Celtics pose for a team portrait in Boston, 1961.
COURTESY OF GETTY IMAGES

The 1962 Finals

EVEN AFTER THE retirement of Bill Sharman, the Celtics remained the best team in the NBA, being the first team to reach 60 wins as the NBA expanded to an 80-game season. Bill Russell won his second consecutive MVP award by averaging 18.9 points and 23.6 rebounds. The road to a fourth consecutive NBA title would be as difficult as ever, as the Celtics were pushed to seven-game series by their old rivals, the Philadelphia Warriors and their newest rivals, the Los Angeles Lakers. Again, the Philadelphia series was an epic struggle, with each team winning alternate games until Game 7 at the Boston Garden. In that game, the Warriors used a big first half from Tom Meschery to take a four-point lead. The Celtics clawed back in the second half, and as usual with these rivals, the game went down to the final seconds. It ended when Sam Jones dribbled around a Russell screen on Tom Gola and swished a one-handed jumper with two seconds left for the series win. The Lakers series would have the same drama when Los Angeles seized a 3–2 lead behind a record 61 points from Elgin Baylor to win Game 5 at the Garden. The Celtics had to win in Los Angeles to force a Game 7, and they rose to the occasion by outscoring the Lakers 62–40 in the second half to win 119–105 behind 35 points from Jones and 20 from Satch Sanders to send the series back to the Garden. Game 7 was another thriller, going to overtime when the Lakers' Frank Selvy missed an open jumper to close regulation. The Celtics prevailed in the extra period, and Russell finished with 30 points and 40 rebounds.

The victorious 1962 Celtics, NBA basketball champions for the fourth consecutive year, whoop it up in the dressing room.
COURTESY OF GETTY IMAGES

October 26, 1963: Celtics Retire Their First Numbers—14 (Cousy) and 22 (Macauley)

ONCE UPON A TIME, the Celtics did not have any retired jerseys. That would change on October 26, 1963, when the club retired the numbers of Bob Cousy (14) and "Easy" Ed Macauley (22) on the same night. Cousy had just retired after the 1962–63 season as the team leader in several statistical categories. He played 13 seasons for the Celtics, reaching the All-Star Game in all of them. He led Boston to six NBA championships and led the league in assists eight times. Macauley did not finish his career in Boston. He was actually traded to the St. Louis Hawks in the deal that netted Bill Russell. But Macauley reached the All-Star Games in all six of his seasons with Boston and he averaged 18.9 points during that span. The retirement of Macauley's jersey began a trend for the Celtics, who retired several jerseys of players who did not play long periods with the team. The Celtics appreciated the contributions of players who made impacts in smaller periods such as Dennis Johnson and Kevin Garnett. Macauley was inducted into the Naismith Memorial Basketball Hall of Fame in 1960, three years before his number was retired.

Ed Macauley (left), coach Red Auerbach (center), and Bob Cousy on September 28, 1953.
COURTESY OF GETTY IMAGES

Bob Cousy

THE IMAGE OF Bob Cousy for today's modern basketball fan is a shorter man with high shorts and Chuck Taylors dribbling with one hand away from defenders to seal a Celtics' win. But there's so much more to Cousy than that. He was one of the league's first great assist men, the consummate point guard who led the early part of the Celtics' dynasty, the first of the NBA. But did you know that Cousy averaged double-figure points in all of his 13 years in Boston, including 20-plus points per game on three occasions? Cousy also led the NBA in assists eight times and was the league's MVP in 1956–57, the Celtics' first championship season. He averaged 20.6. points, 7.5 assists and 4.8 rebounds per game in an era when defenses dominated and shooting percentages were often below 40 percent. Cousy was the NBA's first model point guard, and his impact on the game is unquestionable. He was named to the NBA's Silver anniversary, 35th anniversary, 50th anniversary, and 75th anniversary teams. And at 96 years old, Cousy still closely follows the NBA and the Celtics. Despite a brief comeback with the Cincinnati Royals in 1970, Cousy was inducted into the Naismith Memorial Basketball Hall of Fame in 1971. Cousy also coached the Royals/Kansas City Kings for four seasons in the early 1970s. Finally, the Celtics in 2022 were the first honorees of the Bob Cousy Eastern Conference Champion Trophy when they beat the Miami Heat in a seven-game series.

Bob Cousy poses for a portrait circa 1950 at Boston Arena.

COURTESY OF GETTY IMAGES

Winning It Again in '63

THE CELTICS WERE again the best team in the NBA, winning 58 games in Bob Cousy's final season. The club also welcomed a new face, first-round pick John Havlicek from Ohio State, who finished fourth on the team in scoring. The Celtics' core was still the NBA's best with Sam Jones, Bill Russell, and Tom Heinsohn along with Frank Ramsey, K.C. Jones, and Satch Sanders. There was a new, emerging team in the Eastern Division: the Cincinnati Royals, led by the versatile and brilliant Oscar Robertson, who averaged nearly a triple-double during his third NBA season. The Royals would push the Celtics to seven games in the division finals. In that seventh game, at the Boston Garden, Sam Jones would score a playoff-high 47 points on 18-for-27 shooting, besting Robertson's 43 points, in a 142–131 win. The Celtics again would face the Los Angeles Lakers in the finals. This time Boston would take control behind Russell and Heinsohn, taking a 3–1 lead after four games. Elgin Baylor again burned the Celtics with 43 points to take the series back to Los Angeles for a Game 6. Boston again would display its championship mettle by taking a 14-point halftime lead and then holding on for a 112–109 series-clinching win. Six Celtics scored in double figures, and Russell pulled down 24 rebounds for their fifth consecutive championship.

Tom Heinsohn of the Celtics defends against the Cincinnati Royals' Oscar Robertson.
COURTESY OF GETTY IMAGES

Sixth Time's a Charm

THE 1963–64 CELTICS were perhaps the best team in the Bill Russell era. Boston raced to a 59-win season and again won the Eastern Division with ease. The club picked up Willie Naulls from the San Francisco Warriors for added depth to join the championship core of Bill Russell, Ton Heinsohn, John Havlicek, Satch Sanders, K.C. Jones, Sam Jones, and Frank Ramsey. Again the Celtics matched up with the up-and-coming Cincinnati Royals in the Eastern Division Finals, and defense was the reason the Celtics won in five games. The Celtics held the Royals to 35 percent shooting, including 27 percent from star forward Jerry Lucas. Boston reeled off three straight wins to take control of the series before using 35 rebounds from Russell to reach its eighth consecutive NBA Finals. The opponent was the same, but the city was different. The Celtics took on the San Francisco Warriors, who had relocated from Philadelphia with the same cast, including Wilt Chamberlain, that challenged Boston in years past. Balance was the key to this series. The Celtics battled the Warriors with depth, as eight players averaged at least 6.4 points in the series and six scored in double figures. As usual, Russell won his matchup with Chamberlain, averaging 25.2 rebounds in the series and bringing yet another title back to Boston.

The 1964 World Champion Celtics pose for a team portrait. Seated (left to right): Sam Jones; Frank Ramsey; K. C. Jones; head coach, Red Auerbach; president, Walter A. Brown; Bill Russell; John Havlicek. Standing (left to right): Jack McCarthy; Tom Sanders; Tom Heinsohn; Clyde Lovellette; Willie Naulls; Jim Loscutoff; Larry Siegfried; trainer, Buddy LeRoux; (inset) vice president, Lou Pieri.
COURTESY OF GETTY IMAGES

December 26, 1964: The NBA's First All-Black Starting Five

DURING THE CELTICS' 118–106 Christmas Day win over the Detroit Pistons in 1964, starting forward Tom Heinsohn left with a foot injury that would cause him to miss several games. The next day the Celtics traveled to St. Louis to take on the Hawks, and coach Red Auerbach needed a starter to replace Heinsohn. Instead of John Havlicek, who flourished in a sixth-man role, Auerbach decided on veteran Willie Naulls, who had been a high scorer with the New York Knicks. While Auerbach was trying to assemble his best lineup, he also made history, fielding the first All-Black starting five in NBA history. Bill Russell, Satch Sanders, Sam Jones, K.C. Jones, and Naulls started the next 12 games for the Celtics with Heinsohn out. They won all 12 games. Not only were the Celtics the first team to draft a Black player and hire a Black coach, they broke an unwritten rule that every NBA team would start at least one white player. And this groundbreaking event occurred before the Texas Western University team started five Black players during their NCAA championship game in Kentucky in March 1966. Naulls played his final three seasons with the Celtics and won a championship in each season.

The 1965 World Champion Celtics pose for a team portrait. Seated (left to right): K.C. Jones; Tom Heinsohn; President, Louis Pieri; Head Coach, Red Auerbach; Bill Russell; Sam Jones. Standing (left to right): Ron Bonham; Larry Siegfried; Willie Naullis; Mel Counts; John Thompson; Tom Sanders; John Havlicek; trainer, Buddy LeRoux.

COURTESY OF GETTY IMAGES

John Havlicek, left, and Bill Russell, take a break on the bench during a game against the Philadelphia 76ers, April 15, 1965.
COURTESY OF GETTY IMAGES

Havlicek Steals the Ball

IT WAS APRIL 15, 1965, and the Celtics were battling their rival Philadelphia 76ers in the Eastern Division Finals, seeking a seventh consecutive NBA championship. The series was tight, with each team winning alternate games until Game 7 at Boston Garden. With the Celtics leading 110–109, Bill Russell threw an errant inbounds pass that clipped a wire supporting the basket, giving the 76ers a chance to win with the final possession. Philadelphia guard Hal Greer tried to inbound the ball to superstar center Wilt Chamberlain, but Russell's defense prevented a clean pass. As the five-second count approached, Greer made a toss toward Chet Walker, but Havlicek broke on the ball and knocked it away from Walker into the path of Sam Jones, who retrieved it, dribbled down the floor, and then passed it to Havlicek. Havlicek then tossed the ball toward the Boston basket as time expired, and he was mobbed by celebrating Celtics fans. It became the most iconic call of Celtics announcer Johnny Most's career, as he screamed, "Havlicek steals it! Over to Sam Jones! Havlicek stole the ball! It's all over!" Celtics fans put Havlicek on their shoulders as they carried him off the floor. Although Havlicek was in the third year of his 16-year Hall of Fame career, he would always be known for that steal. And it became one of the more popular plays in NBA history.

Bill Russell: Five MVPs in Eight Years

WHILE BILL RUSSELL was never associated with statistics and numbers as closely as he was with winning, he went on an unprecedented run in the late 1950s and early 1960s of five MVP awards in eight years. Wilt Chamberlain was considered a more imposing physical specimen and dominant player, but Russell was a generational defensive player, one of the best rebounders in NBA history, and a historic winner. Russell won his first MVP in 1957–58, in his second season, when he led the Celtics to the NBA Finals and averaged 16.6 points and 22.7 rebounds per game. He won his second MVP three years later in the midst of the Celtics' title runs, averaging 16.9 points and 23.9 rebounds as the Celtics beat the St. Louis Hawks in the Finals. He won a third MVP award in five years in 1961–62 (18.9 points, 23.6 rebounds) as the Celtics won yet another title. He then became the first NBA player to win three consecutive MVPs (Larry Bird would match that in the 1980s) in 1962–63 in another Celtics championship season. Russell would win his final MVP Award in 1964–65 at age 31 when he averaged 14.1 points and led the NBA in rebounding for the final time in his career with 24.1 per game. It was one of the most remarkable runs by an individual player in NBA history and just one of the reasons why Russell is in the Naismith Basketball Hall of Fame and the greatest Celtic of all time.

Bill Russell #6 and Wilt Chamberlain of the Philadelphia 76ers battle during a game on April 4, 1965 in Boston.
COURTESY OF GETTY IMAGES

March 11, 1965: Bill Russell Pulls Down 49 Rebounds

THERE IS A reason that 55 years after his final NBA game, Bill Russell still ranks second all-time in rebounds with 21,620, trailing only his rival Wilt Chamberlain. Russell was a rebounding machine, and on the night of March 11, 1965, he was stellar at his craft. In a home game against the Detroit Pistons in Providence, Rhode Island, Russell pulled down 49 rebounds in a 112–100 win that improved the Celtics' record to 60–16. Russell also led the Celtics with 27 points on 11-for-24 shooting and added six assists. Russell's 49 rebounds were 39 more than the Pistons' leader, Jackie Moreland, had. Another impressive note was Russell played all 48 minutes. He did not rest. The 1964–65 season, when Russell was 31, was the eighth season of a stellar 10-year run in which he averaged 20 or more rebounds per game. Russell gets deserved credit for his defensive prowess and blocked shots, but he was one of the great rebounders of all time.

Bill Russell #6 rebounds against Bob Warlick #8 of the Detroit Pistons during a game played in 1967 at the Boston Garden.
COURTESY OF GETTY IMAGES

Seventh Straight Title: 1965

IF YOU THOUGHT the Celtics would finally avoid Wilt Chamberlain on their way to a championship, it wasn't happening. In January 1965, the Western Division San Francisco Warriors traded Chamberlain back to his hometown with the Philadelphia 76ers, who had relocated from Syracuse. The Celtics again rolled to an Eastern Division title with a 62–18 record with the same core that had been responsible for the previous titles. Key reserve Frank Ramsey had retired, but K.C. Jones played an expanded role as Boston eliminated the 76ers in a thrilling seven-game series, capped by John Havlicek's famous steal in the final moments of Game 7 to seal another trip to the Finals. The Celtics only outscored the 76ers by 20 points over the seven games, while Chamberlain averaged 30 points and 30 rebounds. But once again, the Celtics' depth and their ability to make key plays late in games made the difference. The Celtics faced the Lakers for the fourth time in seven years in the NBA Finals, which were anticlimactic in comparison to the Philly series. Sam Jones was at his best in this series, averaging nearly 28 points per game, including a 37-point performance in Game 4 as the Celtics took control with a 3–1 lead and gave the home fans another treat by clinching at Boston Garden in Game 5. Russell again was stellar, averaging 17.8 points and 25 rebounds.

Celtics coach Red Auerbach (right), with John Havlicek (center), and Willie Naulls (left) against the Los Angeles Lakers with the Celtics well on their way to a seventh NBA Championship.
COURTESY OF GETTY IMAGES

Jim Loscutoff (LOSCY)

JIM LOSCUTOFF DID not score in bunches. He was not one of the Celtics' superstars, but he was an indispensable piece of the early championship teams with his defense, hustle, and physical play. Loscutoff (nicknamed Loscy) played eight-plus seasons with the Celtics, winning seven championships as one of Red Auerbach's enforcers in the paint. Loscutoff collected a career-high 26 rebounds during his rookie season and also sank one of the biggest free throws in Celtics history. That free throw in Game 7 of the 1957 NBA championship against the St. Louis Hawks gave the Celtics their first NBA title, earning Loscutoff a place in Celtics lore.

Loscutoff was the third overall pick in the 1955 draft out of the University of Oregon. Celtics coach Red Auerbach was given sage advice from University of Washington assistant coach Bob Donham, a former Celtic, who suggested Loscutoff would be the perfect fit. In 511 games, Loscutoff averaged 6.2 points and 5.6 rebounds. The Celtics offered to retire Loscutoff's No. 18, but he humbly refused. He said he wanted future players to wear 18, and one future great Celtic did: Dave Cowens. The Celtics held a ceremony in April 1977 to honor Loscutoff, and instead of raising his number into the rafters, his nickname "Loscy" was lifted amongst the retired numbers. Loscutoff was brought to tears.

James Loscutoff poses for a mock action portrait circa 1955 in Boston.
COURTESY OF GETTY IMAGES

Red's Final Run: 1966

THE CELTICS WERE an aging team in 1966, and top scorer Tom Heinsohn decided to retire to pursue the insurance business, leaving the club without significant offense. But John Havlicek and Larry Siegfried—as well as Don Nelson, who was signed from the Los Angeles Lakers—kept the Celtics solid offensively. The mark of this team was defense, as Boston led the league in opponent's scoring, thanks in large part to Bill Russell. Since the Celtics were edged out by the 76ers in the Eastern Division, they were forced to play Cincinnati in the semifinal round to meet the 76ers in the division final. The road team won every game in the series until the Celtics used 34 points from Sam Jones and 31 rebounds from Russell to win Game 5 in Boston. Jones and Havlicek combined to knock the 76ers out in five games, despite another monster series from Chamberlain, including 46 points and 34 rebounds in Game 5. The Finals against the Lakers was another epic seven-game series, but this time the Celtics raced to a 3–1 lead only to watch Jerry West and Elgin Baylor lead Los Angeles to consecutive wins to force Game 7. The Celtics took a big lead and were cruising, prompting Auerbach to light his victory cigar with Massachusetts governor John Volpe before the buzzer sounded. Leroy Ellis's jumper with just seconds left cut the Celtics' lead to two points, but K.C. Jones dribbled out the clock for championship number eight in a row. Auerbach announced his retirement from coaching shortly afterward.

Arnold "Red" Auerbach receives help from former teammate Bill Russell in raising his retiring Boston Celtics team jersey number.
COURTESY OF GETTY IMAGES

Russell vs. Chamberlain

BEFORE MAGIC VS. BIRD or Ali vs. Frazier, Bill Russell vs. Wilt Chamberlain was the greatest one-on-one sports rivalry. They were two titans at the center position. Russell was a 6-foot-9-inch workhorse who compensated for his lack of height and size with hustle and grit. Chamberlain was the once-in-a-lifetime talent who blended his imposing size with speed and grace around the basket. He was an intimidating figure, but also a high-jump champion with the athleticism and prowess to score at will. The two met six times in the Eastern Division Finals between the Celtics and the Philadelphia Warriors/76ers, and Russell won five of those matchups. Russell faced Chamberlain twice in the NBA Finals: in 1964 against Chamberlain's San Francisco Warriors and in 1969 against Wilt's Lakers. Russell's team won both. While Chamberlain posted the most impressive stats, such as 30.1 points and 31.4 rebounds in the 1964–65 Eastern Division Finals, Russell always seemed to have the better team. The two men were friends, often dining together during series or visiting each other's homes on road trips, but once they were on the floor, they battled valiantly. Russell got the final victory in their rivalry, in the 1969 Finals when the Celtics eked out a Game 7 win over the Lakers in Inglewood. Chamberlain was not on the floor during the final minutes, leaving in the fourth quarter with a knee injury with coach Butch Van Breda Kolff refusing to put him back in. Russell was quoted as saying he would never have asked out of a Finals game because of an injury.

Bill Russell #6 on his way to the basket drives pass Wilt Chamberlain #13 of the Philadelphia 76ers during a game at the Boston Garden.
COURTESY OF GETTY IMAGES

Bill Russell Becomes First Black Coach

THE CELTICS HAVE taken pride in being a franchise that broke barriers. They drafted the NBA's first Black player in Chuck Cooper in 1950, and 14 years later they fielded the first Black starting five. When Red Auerbach decided to conclude his 16-year tenure and name a new coach, he only looked a few feet down the bench for his replacement as the Celtics selected five-time MVP Bill Russell. Russell did not retire as a player, however, meaning he became the sport's first Black player-coach. Auerbach considered Frank Ramsey, Bob Cousy, and Tom Heinsohn, but he decided on Russell. On April 16, 1966, before the Celtics took on the Los Angeles Lakers for their eighth consecutive title, Russell was named head coach for the 1966–67 season. Russell was the first Black coach in modern-day professional sports and made the adjustment to supervise players who were also his teammates. Russell told reporters he would have no issue relating to players regardless of their race because of his basketball knowledge and ability to communicate. Russell coached the Celtics for three seasons, stepping down after his final championship season in 1968–69. He would return to coach the Seattle SuperSonics in the 1970s and Sacramento Kings in the late 1980s.

Celtics player-coach Bill Russell, March 17, 1968.

COURTESY OF GETTY IMAGES

The Glue Guy, K.C. Jones

K.C. JONES PLAYED just nine seasons in the NBA and never averaged more than 9.2 points per game, but he was essential to the Celtics' dynasty. Jones was one of the league's top defenders, accepting the assignment of guarding the opposing team's best player. While the Celtics had scorers such as Bob Cousy, Bill Russell, and Sam Jones, K.C. Jones made his name with defense, and he jumped into the Celtics rotation as a 26-year-old rookie. He won eight championships in his nine seasons, retiring after the Celtics lost to the Philadelphia 76ers in the Eastern Division Finals in 1967. As a player, Jones was inducted into the Naismith Basketball Hall of Fame in 1989 for his contributions to the Celtics and also for winning two national championships with the University of San Francisco as a teammate of Russell. Jones may be better remembered for his impact as a coach, leading the Washington Bullets to the NBA Finals in 1975 and then returning to Boston to lead the Celtics to titles in 1984 and 1986. But his impact as a player is unquestioned because it went beyond the stat sheet.

Portrait of KC Jones kneeling and palming a basketball during his time playing for the Celtics, San Francisco, California, 1980.
COURTESY OF GETTY IMAGES

The Streak Ends

THE CELTICS HAD dominated the NBA since they acquired Bill Russell in a draft-day trade. Boston ruled professional basketball with eight consecutive championships, and the Celtics dominated even after the departures of Bob Cousy and Bill Sharman. Those cornerstones were replaced with John Havlicek, Don Nelson, and Sam Jones. In five of those eight championship runs, the Celtics beat the Philadelphia Warriors or Philadelphia 76ers. It was a rivalry that Boston commanded as Russell would win his matchup with Wilt Chamberlain, who played for the Warriors in Philadelphia and later in San Francisco. In 1965, Chamberlain was traded back to Philadelphia, who were now the 76ers after moving from Syracuse. The Celtics ran into the 76ers in the 1967 Eastern Division Finals but were no match, losing in five games. Chamberlain could not be stopped in this series, averaging a triple-double (21.6 points, 32 rebounds and 10 assists). The Celtics fell behind 3–0 in the series, coming back for a 121–117 Game 4 win behind 32 points from Jones and 28 rebounds from Russell, but the 76ers won Game 5 to end the Celtics' eight-year reign. It was the first year for Russell as player-coach after Red Auerbach had been elevated to team president. Russell would atone for this defeat with consecutive championships.

John Havlicek #17 drives the ball against the Philadelphia 76ers during a game played in 1967 at the Boston Garden.
COURTESY OF GETTY IMAGES

Coming Back to Win in '68

THE CELTICS WATCHED their streak of eight consecutive championships come to an abrupt end at the hands of the rival Philadelphia 76ers, who beat Boston in the Eastern Division Finals before beating the San Francisco Warriors for their first NBA title. With a full squad returning, the 76ers were the favorites to repeat in 1968. The Celtics were watching their dynasty slowly dissolve. Bill Russell, now the coach, was aging as a player. Players such as Sam Jones were near the ends of their careers while Tom Heinsohn had retired. Still, the Celtics had talent, such as bruising forward Bailey Howell and a supporting cast of Larry Siegfried, Satch Sanders, and Don Nelson. The Celtics won 54 games, but finished eight games behind the 76ers. But that mattered little when the postseason began. After beating the Detroit Pistons in the first round, the Celtics faced the 76ers in another epic series. Trailing the series 3–1 and without home-court advantage, the Celtics stormed back to win the final three games, including a 100–96 victory in Game 7. Russell and Havlicek played all 48 minutes in that game. After such as a struggle with the 76ers, the Celtics made easier work of the Los Angeles Lakers in the Finals, winning in six games, despite brilliant series from Jerry West and Elgin Baylor. Boston won the final two games of the series, with Havlicek scoring 40 points in the clinching Game 6. Six players scored in double figures during the series, showing the balance the team had established as the dynasty progressed.

Jerry West #44 of the Los Angeles Lakers looks to make a move against John Havlicek #17 during a game played in 1968 at the Boston Garden.
COURTESY OF GETTY IMAGES

Russell's Final Run in 1969

THE CELTICS DYNASTY of 11 titles in 13 years was coming to a close. Bill Russell was 34 and starting to show fatigue as a coach and player, and he was showing more interest in social activism. The core of those championship teams was also aging, with Satch Sanders and Sam Jones in their final years. Unexpectedly, the Celtics limped through the regular season, finishing 48–34 and fourth in the Eastern Division, making their chances of even reaching the NBA Finals slim. Yet, with Russell gathering all of his energy and guile and his teammates still possessing that championship culture, the Celtics made an improbable run, beating the rival Philadelphia 76ers, this time without Wilt Chamberlain, in the first round and then topping the emerging New York Knicks in the Eastern Division Finals. The next opponent was a familiar one in the Los Angeles Lakers, this time with Chamberlain, who had been acquired before the 1968 season. The Lakers won Games 1 and 2, with Jerry West averaging 47 points.The Celtics responded with two home wins before the Lakers won Game 5. With their season and legacy at stake, the Celtics edged the Lakers 99–90 in Russell's last game at the Boston Garden. He pulled down 19 rebounds. In an epic Game 7, the Lakers and Celtics battled until the final minutes before Don Nelson's clinching jumper, a ball that hit back rim, soared in the air and fell right through the hoop. The Celtics held on, winning 108–106 and turning Russell into a champion again as he retired soon after.

Fans gather at Boston's City Hall Plaza for the Celtics' NBA Championship victory parade on May 8, 1969.
COURTESY OF GETTY IMAGES

As Em Bryant #7 and Rich Johnson begin to celebrate, Jerry West #44 of the Lakers walks off the court after the Celtics beat them in Game 7 at the Inglewood Forum on May 5, 1969 in Los Angeles.
COURTESY OF GETTY IMAGES

That Epic Game 7

THE CELTICS AND Lakers wouldn't meet in the NBA Finals for another 15 years following their thrilling Game 7 in the 1969 finals at the Inglewood Forum. The Lakers were the favored team and had won the first two games of the series before the Celtics rallied to win three of the next four, including Bill Russell's final home game in Game 6. The deciding game was controlled by the Celtics, who jumped out to a 15-point lead and staved off rallies until the final minutes. Wilt Chamberlain, acquired from the Philadelphia 76ers, left the game with a knee injury with five minutes left and the Lakers rallying. Chamberlain asked back into the game, but coach Butch Van Breda Kolff refused to put him back in, leaving the Lakers shorthanded. With the Celtics leading 103–102, Don Nelson launched a jumper that caromed high off the rim and nestled through the basket for the clinching score. The Lakers furious rally fell short, despite 42 points by the great Jerry West and 18 points and 27 rebounds from Chamberlain. Russell, in his final NBA game, pulled down 19 rebounds, and John Havlicek led the Celtics with 26 points. Sam Jones, also in his final NBA game, added 24 points before fouling out. The Celtics had been the fourth seed in the Eastern Division and made an improbable run to their 11th championship. West was named MVP of the series, but the Celtics won as a team, getting 20 points from unheralded guard Em Bryant, finishing the Russell era in style.

Sam Jones #24 dribbles the ball up court against the Philadelphia 76ers in 1965 at Convention Hall in Philadelphia.
COURTESY OF GETTY IMAGES

The Stellar Sam Jones

WHILE HE IS a Hall of Famer and was one of the great scorers of the 1960s, Sam Jones is often overlooked in discussions of NBA history. The Celtics would not have racked up 11 championships between 1957 and 1969 without Jones, who was the smooth scoring, workhorse guard who got better as he aged, averaging 20-plus points in his age 31 through 34 seasons, including 21.3 points at age 34, when he was named to his fifth All-Star Game. Jones was originally a draft pick of the rival Minneapolis Lakers in 1956 but chose to return to college and fulfill military commitments. Red Auerbach was scouting talent in North Carolina and was told the state's best talent was at tiny North Carolina College (now North Carolina Central). It was Jones, and Auerbach selected him eighth overall without actually having seen him play. Jones got off to a slow start of his career, playing just 10 minutes per game as a rookie. But his role expanded as the Celtics' became a league power. Eventually, Jones became a staple at shooting guard, with K.C. Jones joining the backcourt as a defensive ace. They were the supporting cast for Bill Russell and Bob Cousy, and Sam Jones's role expanded once Bill Sharman and Cousy departed. Jones's finest moment was in his final NBA game, when he scored 24 points to lead the Celtics over the Lakers in Game 7 of the NBA Finals. He would become a substitute teacher after retirement.

The New Celtics Era: Here Come Cowens and White

AFTER THE CELTICS won the championship in 1969, the franchise began a transformation with Bill Russell and Sam Jones retiring. The core of the championship teams was all gone. John Havlicek, Satch Sanders, and Don Nelson remained, but they needed help. The resurgence began with the drafting of Jo Jo White, a scoring guard from the University of Kansas who helped America win gold on the 1968 Olympic team. White was the type of cornerstone player who could lead the Celtics into the next decade, and he was fourth on the team in scoring as a rookie. The rebuild continued in 1970, when the Celtics landed the fourth pick in the NBA Draft after a 34–48 season and no postseason appearance. The Celtics selected Florida State center Dave Cowens. Cowens would turn into a fiery leader, an undersized big man who battled with the likes of Abdul-Jabbar and Walton and eventually became the team's second player-coach. White and Cowens would combine with Havlicek to lead Boston to titles in 1974 and 1976 and help the franchise continue its dominance after the departure of Russell. They were considered the first Big Three for the Celtics. Cowens and White were each inducted into the Naismith Memorial Basketball Hall of Fame, a testament to their impact on the franchise. A second version of the Big Three would arrive in the 1980s.

(From left) John Havlicek, JoJo White, and Dave Cowens stand with head coach Tom Heinsohn. The Celtics hosted the Chicago Bulls in a regular season game at the Boston Garden on January 9, 1974.

COURTESY OF GETTY IMAGES

Cowens Wins Rookie of the Year

DAVE COWENS IMMEDIATELY made an impact with the Celtics, winning co-Rookie of the Year with Portland's Geoff Petrie. Cowens was thrust into the starting lineup by coach Tom Heinsohn. He finished that first season with the Celtics averaging 17 points and 15 rebounds and emerging as the best in what was a stellar 1970–71 rookie class that included Bob Lanier, Pete Maravich, Rudy Tomjanovich, Sam Lacey, Calvin Murphy, and Nate Archibald. Cowens's best game of his rookie season came on February 28, 1971, when he scored 36 points and pulled down 19 rebounds in a loss to the Milwaukee Bucks. Cowens scored in double figures in 70 of his 81 games and recorded double-digit rebounds in 72 games. He also collected 20 or more rebounds in 14 games and grabbed 28 in a loss at Philadelphia on February 2, 1971. He finished seventh in the NBA in rebounding in 1970–71. He would win the league's MVP award two years later.

Dave Cowens shoots against the Washington Bullets during a game at the Capital Center in Baltimore, circa 1970.
COURTESY OF GETTY IMAGES

Losing in the 1973 Eastern Conference Finals

FOUR YEARS AFTER winning their 11th NBA championship and then embarking on a rebuild, the Celtics were back on top of the NBA. The 1972–73 squad finished with the best record in the league at 68–14. Dave Cowens, who averaged 20.5 points and 16.2 rebounds per game, was named league MVP. Four players averaged in double figures, led by John Havlicek's 23.8 points. Bruising forward Paul Silas averaged a double-double. Coach Tommy Heinsohn would insist this was the best team he had ever coached.

After disposing of the Atlanta Hawks in the Eastern semifinals, the Celtics ran into a growing dynasty in the New York Knicks, who had won the NBA title in 1970 and lost to the Lakers in 1972. The Knicks finished 11 games behind the Celtics in the Atlantic Division, yet the Celtics had trouble in their conference finals matchup. They could do little to stop future Hall of Famer Walt Frazier, who averaged 26.1 points and shot nearly 52 percent in the seven games. Every game in the series alternated home court; the Celtics trailed three games to one but rallied to force a Game 7 at home. In that deciding game, the Celtics were cold from the field, shooting 37.3 percent and getting just four points from Havlicek. The Knicks outscored the Celtics 53–35 in the second and third periods, cruising to a 94–78 win. Havlicek had badly injured his right shoulder in Game 4, limiting his production during the final three games. Heinsohn said a healthy Havlicek would have helped the Celtics in that series. Instead, they were eliminated but motivated to make another run in 1974.

Bill Bradley #24 of the New York Knicks moves the ball against John Havlicek during a game played in 1973 at the Boston Garden.
COURTESY OF GETTY IMAGES

Coach Tommy Heinsohn

TOMMY HEINSOHN RETIRED after the Celtics won the championship in 1964–65 to sell insurance. He turned down an opportunity to coach Bill Russell in 1966, and Russell was named player-coach for his final three seasons. When Russell retired from playing, he also retired from coaching to enter broadcasting, leaving the Celtics with an opening. Enter Heinsohn. He took over as coach for the 1969–70 season, a real transition period for the Celtics. Russell and Sam Jones retired, leaving John Havlicek as the franchise cornerstone with a bunch of aging veterans. After the Celtics missed the playoffs in two consecutive seasons for the second time in franchise history, Heinsohn led the club on another impressive run, although it wasn't as dominant as in the 1960s, when the NBA had nine teams. As the league had grown, the talent base increased and it became more difficult to win. The Celtics went to the playoffs in six consecutive seasons, and they won 68 games in 1973. Heinsohn led the Celtics' first Big Three—Jo Jo White, Dave Cowens, and John Havlicek—to NBA titles in 1974 and 1976, the team's first titles without Russell. He finished with a career winning percentage of 61.9 percent, was named NBA Coach of the Year in 1972–73, and was inducted into the Naismith Memorial Basketball Hall of Fame in 2015 as a coach. He already had been inducted into the Hall of Fame as a player in 1986. Heinsohn helped the Celtics move forward after the Russell years, and then he became a wildly successful analyst after he departed in 1978 until his death in 2020.

Head coach Tom Heinsohn looks on during an NBA game circa 1970–78 at the Boston Garden.
COURTESY OF GETTY IMAGES

Jo Jo White

A MAIN CONTRIBUTOR to the Celtics resurgence in the 1970s was point guard Jo Jo White, taken with Boston's first-round pick in 1969 out of the University of Kansas. A 1968 Olympian, White stabilized the Boston backcourt and became a staple there for a decade, helping the club to two championships and forming the original Big Three with Dave Cowens and John Havlicek. In 10 seasons with the Celtics, he averaged 18.4 points, 5.1 assists, and 4.3 rebounds per game. He was named to seven All-Star Games, was two-time All-NBA, and was part of the 1969–70 All-Rookie Team. White saved his best basketball for the monumental moments, especially the 1976 Finals, when he averaged 21.7 points, 5.8 assists and 4.3 rebounds per game as the Celtics disposed of the Phoenix Suns in six games. As the NBA expanded in the late 1960s and the talent pool increased, there was uncertainty whether the Celtics would ever return to their past glory, but White was one of the central figures of the franchise's rebirth following the retirement of Bill Russell. A rebuilding Celtics team traded White to the Golden State Warriors for a first-round pick in 1979, and he then finished his career with the Kansas City Kings. However, White will always be known as an all-time great Celtic, and he was inducted into the Naismith Memorial Basketball Hall of Fame in 2015 after surviving brain surgery. White passed away in 2018.

Close up of Jo Jo White.
COURTESY OF GETTY IMAGES

Dave Cowens

Dave Cowens #18 and John Havlicek chat during an NBA game circa 1970s at the Boston Garden.
COURTESY OF GETTY IMAGES

BACK WHEN NBA centers were mammoth, they planted themselves in the paint, ate up rebounds, blocked shots, and knocked down any guard who dared drive for a layup without fear of a flagrant foul. At 6-foot-9, Dave Cowens battled with those behemoths nightly. Cowens was an undersized but gutsy big man taken fourth overall out of Florida State in 1970, and he became a Celtics' staple for the next decade, going at it with the Waltons, Laniers, Abdul-Jabbars, and Reeds while helping Boston to two NBA championships in his tenure Cowens was named the 1971 NBA Rookie of the Year, averaging 17 points and 15 rebounds per game, was named to eight All-Star Games, and was voted the 1973 NBA MVP. Cowens wowed Boston faithful with his hustle and guile and also his no-nonsense style. Cowens left the Celtics briefly in 1977 because of issues with management but eventually returned and produced a double-double season in 1977–78. After coach Satch Sanders was fired after a 2–12 start in 1978–79, Cowens took over as the team's second player coach—a role that Bill Russell had filled a decade earlier. In his final season in Boston, Cowens played with a rookie named Larry Bird, averaging 14.2 points and 8.1 rebounds per game on that 1979–80 team. Cowens eventually retired, but returned after a two-year absence to play 40 games with the Milwaukee Bucks. Cowens was inducted into the Naismith Memorial Basketball Hall of Fame in 1991 and was named to the NBA's all-time 50th- and 75th-anniversary teams.

Paul Silas

THE CELTICS LACKED a physical power forward to join Dave Cowens in the paint in the early 1970s. Paul Silas was a bruising big man who had played eight seasons in the NBA and was named to the 1972 NBA All-Star team. Just after the 1972 season, the Celtics agreed to acquire Silas from the Phoenix Suns for Charlie Scott, who would actually return to Boston a few years later. Silas gave Cowens a partner in the Celtics frontcourt, and the club achieved great success during his four seasons in Boston, winning two championships and making two appearances in the Eastern Conference Finals. Silas had the ability to score in the paint, could rebound with bigger players, and was one of the more durable players in the NBA. Silas played 80 or more games in his final 10 NBA seasons, including 82 in his final year in 1979–80. Silas was also the king of the double-double, averaging double figures in points and rebounds in eight of his first 12 NBA seasons. Silas was fourth in the NBA in rebounding in 1975–76, his last season in Boston, as the Celtics bested his former team, the Suns, for the title. Just before the 1976–77 season began, the Celtics traded Silas to the Denver Nuggets in a three-team deal that brought back Detroit's Curtis Rowe—an unpopular move that contributed to the end of the Celtics' 1970s run. Silas would win another championship in 1979 with the Seattle SuperSonics. Silas, whose son Stephen was recently coach of the Houston Rockets, passed away in 2022.

Paul Silas, left, shares a laugh with team president and general manager Red Auerbach on the opening day of Celtics training camp at the Mass Maritime Academy in 1974.
COURTESY OF GETTY IMAGES

Cowens Wins 1973 NBA MVP

GENERALLY, IT TAKES longer than three seasons to emerge as the NBA's best player. That wasn't the case for Dave Cowens, who led the Celtics to a franchise-best 68 wins in 1972–73 en route to the MVP Award in just his third NBA season. Cowens averaged 20.5 points, 16.2 rebounds, and 4.1 assists per game (blocked shots were not a recorded stat until the next season). Cowens was one of the primary players behind the Celtics' resurgence in the 1970s following the retirement of Bill Russell. Undersized for a center, Cowens battled bigger players and was a rebounding menace. During the MVP season, Cowens scored 30 or more points nine times, including 38 on December 26, 1972, against the New York Knicks. On March 20, 1973, Cowens pulled down a career-high 32 rebounds and scored 20 points in a 94–89 win over the Houston Rockets. As for durability, Cowens played 48 or more minutes eight times during that season, and he played 40 or more minutes in 55 of his league-leading 82 games. That 1972–73 Celtics club appeared headed for their first championship since the Russell era, but John Havlicek suffered a shoulder injury during the Eastern Conference Finals and the Celtics lost in seven games to the New York Knicks. Cowens would help Boston win the championship in two of the next three seasons, but in 1973 he was at his absolute best.

Dave Cowens holds his MVP trophy while standing with Tommy Heinsohn prior to a game in 1973 at the Boston Garden.
COURTESY OF GETTY IMAGES

Returning to Prominence in 1974

IRONICALLY, THE 1973–74 Celtics were 12 games worse than the previous year's team in the regular season. After winning a franchise-best 68 games 1972–73, the Celtics won the Atlantic with 56 wins the following year, finishing seven games better than the defending champion New York Knicks. This edition of the Celtics featured a balanced attack, with six players averaging in double figures, led by John Havlicek, who was completely healthy after that shoulder injury in 1973. The Celtics were able to get by the upstart Buffalo Braves in the first round of the playoffs, winning their first-round series in six games. Next was a rematch with the Knicks, who had knocked off the Celtics in seven games the year before. This matchup would not be so close. Boston punched first, winning the first two games of the series, before losing Game 3. Havlicek, in the midst of a remarkable playoff run, scored 69 points over the final two games to close out the series. The Celtics would face a new foe in the NBA Finals, the Milwaukee Bucks and their center Kareem Abdul-Jabbar, looking for his second title in four years. The Celtics had a chance to close out the series in Game 6, but Abdul-Jabbar swished one of his patented sky-hooks in double-overtime to win the game for the Bucks. But the Celtics, again showing their championship mettle, traveled back to Milwaukee and dominated Game 7 as Dave Cowens scored 28 points and Paul Silas and Paul Westphal combined for 26 in a 102–87 win. It was the Celtics' first title in five years, and their first without Bill Russell. Havlicek was named Finals MVP.

John Havlicek (left) and Jo Jo White, celebrate winning the 1974 NBA Championship at the Milwaukee Arena.
COURTESY OF GETTY IMAGES

The 1974 Championship, Game 7

THE CELTICS FELT as if they had blown an opportunity in 1973; after racing to the number one seed in the Eastern Conference with 68 wins, they were tripped up by the New York Knicks in the Eastern Conference Finals. The 1974 Finals was an epic series against a great opponent in the Milwaukee Bucks, a team that featured all-time greats Kareem Abdul-Jabbar and Oscar Robertson. The series went to a seventh game at Milwaukee Arena, with the Celtics as the underdogs. Boston had been historically flawless in Game 7s, and this one was no different. The Celtics made the calculated gamble of fronting Abdul-Jabbar, meaning putting a defender in front of him to make it for difficult for his teammates to pass the ball to the big man. Kareem still had 26 points and 13 rebounds, but the Celtics would take those numbers considering he averaged 33 points in the series. Boston's defense took over in the first half, forcing 11 turnovers as it raced to a 53–40 lead. Milwaukee rallied in the third quarter to slice the lead to 81–76, but the Celtics restored order in the fourth, going on a 10–0 run to take complete control. Rookie Paul Westphal helped out with his defense, while Paul Silas scored 14 points with nine rebounds off the bench. The Celtics had returned to glory after a five-year wait.

Milwaukee Bucks' Cornell Warner grabs a rebound in front of Boston Celtics John Havlicek and #19 Don Nelson in the first quarter of the Bucks–Celtics NBA championship game.

COURTESY OF GETTY IMAGES

Falling Short in '75

THE CELTICS basically ran it back with the same squad that won in 1974, and they again clinched the Atlantic Division with 60 wins despite Dave Cowens missing 17 regular-season games. The Washington Bullets, coached by former Celtic K.C. Jones, won the Central Division with 60 wins and were the main obstacle. The Celtics had major trouble with Bullets' size in the Eastern Conference Finals—they could do little to stop future Hall of Famer Elvin Hayes and guard Phil Chenier, while veteran Wes Unseld averaged nearly 17 rebounds in the series. The Celtics shot just 40.3 percent from the field in the series, including sub-40 percent from Dave Cowens and John Havlicek. The Celtics' core was beginning to age, with Havlicek and Don Nelson each having turned 34 during the season. In the deciding game, the Celtics' starters besides Cowens shot 19-for-61 from the field and they lost 98–92 in Landover, Maryland. The Celtics knew they were a few players short of getting back to the title, and they would make the necessary moves for the 1975–76 season.

Don Nelson #19 battles for the ball against Elvin Hayes #11 of the Washington Bullets during a game played in 1975 at the Boston Garden.

COURTESY OF GETTY IMAGES

The Celtics Acquire Charlie Scott

BEFORE HE came to Boston in 1975, Charlie Scott was a player who was considered temperamental, mercurial, and perhaps too selfish to contribute to a winning team. That was never the case during his time with the Celtics, when he was the key addition for the 1976 championship team. Scott was a prolific scorer during his first two seasons in the ABA with the Virginia Squires and then with the Phoenix Suns. But the swingman also was unhappy with losing, and it became an issue with Phoenix Suns coach John McLeod. Celtics president Red Auerbach and coach Tom Heinsohn thought the club needed a spark after losing in the Eastern Conference Finals to the Washington Bullets and decided to take a chance on Scott, moving promising guard Paul Westphal to Phoenix in the deal. Scott became the consummate teammate, working within Heinsohn's system and becoming an impact defender for the 1975–76 Celtics. Scott was third on the club in scoring behind Dave Cowens and Jo Jo White and gave some relief to an aging John Havlicek in the backcourt. Winning cured all Scott's issues, as he was considered the perfect addition to a team that needed one more piece. Scott was inducted into the Naismith Memorial Basketball Hall of Fame in 2018 and is revered in Boston for his contributions to that title team.

Charlie Scott goes up for a layup during a game at the Capital Centre in Landover, Maryland, circa 1975.
COURTESY OF GETTY IMAGES

The Don Nelson Impact

ONE OF THE threads that connected the Celtics' glory days of the 1960s with the two championships in the 1970s was Don Nelson. Before he became a Hall of Fame NBA coach, Nelson was a key contributor on five championship teams with his pinpoint shooting and solid rebounding. Nelson was drafted in 1962 by the Chicago Packers (who eventually became the Zephyrs before moving to Baltimore). He spent a season there before being placed on waivers and picked up by the Los Angeles Lakers. After two seasons with the Lakers, he signed as a free agent with the Celtics before the 1965–66 season. After averaging just 2.4 points per game in his final season with the Lakers, Nelson boosted his scoring average to 10.2 in helping the Celtics to another NBA championship. Nelson saved his best basketball for the playoffs. Of course, he is known for the famous Nelson bounce, a jumper in Game 7 of the 1969 NBA Finals that bounced high off the back of the rim and fell through the hoop for a clinching basket against the Lakers. In 134 playoff games, Nelson shot 50 percent from the field as the Celtics won 20 of his 26 series. Nelson retired after the Celtics won their second title in three seasons in 1976, and his No. 19 was retired by Boston on December 15, 1976.

Don Nelson shoots a free throw against the Los Angeles Lakers, circa 1967 at the Boston Garden.
COURTESY OF GETTY IMAGES

John Havlicek #17 shoots against Ricky Sobers #40 of the Phoenix Suns during Game Five of the NBA Finals. The Celtics defeated the Phoenix Suns 128–126 in triple overtime and would later win the series 4–2 to capture the 1976 NBA Championship.
COURTESY OF GETTY IMAGES

Game 5 of the 1976 Finals: Celtics Win in 3 OT

IN ONE OF the most exciting games in NBA Finals history, the Celtics and Phoenix Suns battled for control of the series in Game 5 at Boston Garden. The Celtics believed they had won the game in double overtime on John Havlicek's bank shot that appeared to beat the buzzer for a 111–110 win—but the shot had actually gone through the net at the two-second mark. The crowd rushed the floor in celebration, and one fan igniting an altercation with official Richie Powers. The two wrestled at midcourt before being separated. The officials and police not only had to clear the floor, but they also call the Celtics back from the locker room to finish the final second of the second overtime. Officials decided to give the Suns one second of time. With no timeouts left and down one point, the Suns called a timeout, were assessed a technical foul, resulting in a Celtics free throw, but then received the ball back at half court with a better chance of scoring. Garfield Heard drained an 18-footer at the buzzer to shock a Celtics crowd that was ready to storm the court again, sending the game to a third overtime. In the third stanza, the Celtics took control with consecutive buckets from reserve Glenn McDonald, who also grabbed a key rebound with Dave Cowens on the bench after fouling out. The Suns cut the deficit to two points with 12 seconds left, but the Celtics closed out the game by passing the ball away from Suns defenders until Jo Jo White dribbled out the clock for the thrilling win.

Cedric Maxwell #31 passes against Rick Mahorn #44 of the Washington Bullets during a game played in 1982 at the Boston Garden.
COURTESY OF GETTY IMAGES

Celtics Draft Cedric Maxwell

HE WAS NICKNAMED "Cornbread" after the character played by Jamaal Wilkes in the movie *Cornbread, Earl and Me*, and that name has stuck for more than 40 years. Maxwell was the Celtics' first-round draft pick (12th overall) out of UNC Charlotte in 1977, a versatile forward who became the heart and soul of those early 1980s Celtics teams, and the MVP of the 1981 NBA Finals. After being a reserve during his rookie season, Maxwell jumped into the starting lineup in 1978–79 and became an impact player, averaging 19 points and nearly 10 rebounds per game. When highly-heralded Larry Bird joined the club in 1979, he teamed with Maxwell for an imposing starting frontcourt along with center Robert Parish a year later. In 1981, Maxwell was the best player on the floor for the Celtics during the championship series against the Houston Rockets. Maxwell averaged 17.7 points and 9.5 rebounds and shot 56.8 percent from the field to bring Boston its first title in five years. Three years later, in the NBA Finals against the Los Angeles Lakers, Maxwell was an infamous trash talker who used his words to get into the heads of Lakers players James Worthy and Michael Cooper in helping the Celtics to a second title in four years. Maxwell played eight seasons for the Celtics before being traded to the Los Angeles Clippers. He returned to Boston to become a popular radio analyst, and the Celtics retired his No. 31 on December 15, 2003.

John Havlicek is honored during halftime of his last game of professional basketball after 16 years with the Boston Celtics on April 9, 1978 at the Boston Garden.
COURTESY OF GETTY IMAGES

Hondo Calls It Quits

JOHN HAVLICEK, PERHAPS because of his low-key demeanor and style, is not always mentioned among the greatest Celtics of all time. That list is likely whittled down to Larry Bird and Bill Russell. But Havlicek could easily be considered the third player on that list, finishing as the Celtics' all-time leading scorer with 26,395 points, all of which he scored without the option of a 3-point shot. Havlicek played 16 seasons, all with the Celtics, and reached the All-Star Game 13 times. In his final NBA season at age 37, Havlicek played in all 82 games and averaged 16 points. He helped the Celtics to eight championships, was the 1974 NBA Finals MVP, and was named to the NBA's 35th anniversary, 50th anniversary, and 75th anniversary teams. He was the critical connection between the 1960s dynasty and the two championships in the 1970s. And he notched the greatest steal in NBA history when he intercepted a Philadelphia inbounds pass to secure the Celtics' Game 7 victory over the 76ers in the 1965 Eastern Division Finals. He also owned the Celtics' season scoring average record of 28.9 points for 17 years until it was broken by Larry Bird. Havlicek was named to eight All-Defensive teams for his ability to hawk the ball and get steals. He was inducted into the Naismith Memorial Basketball Hall of Fame, and the Celtics retired his No. 17 on October 13, 1978. Havlicek returned to Boston for many reunions and celebrations before his passing in 2019.

The Larry Bird Draft

THE CELTICS WERE in chaos in 1977–78, losing 50 games and missing the playoffs entirely. The silver lining was that they were granted the sixth pick in the 1978 NBA Draft. Red Auerbach, always the astute thinker, took the long-term approach with this draft, taking Indiana State University forward Larry Bird with the team's first-round pick. However, there was a catch: Bird would not come to the club until the 1979–80 season. Bird was eligible for the draft because his college class had completed four years (Bird had transferred to Indiana State from Indiana) but he decided to return to Indiana State for his senior year. Teams that picked ahead of the Celtics, such as the Indiana Pacers and Portland Trail Blazers, couldn't entice Bird to leave school, so they drafted elsewhere. Auerbach was willing to wait a year, so he took Bird despite his team needing help after a 32-win season. Auerbach viewed Bird as a franchise cornerstone, a generational player, and he was willing to sacrifice the next season to get Bird in Celtics green. The 1978–79 team was even worse than the year before, with 18 different players suiting up and the team going through two coaches. But help would soon arrive, as Bird led his Indiana State team to the national championship game before reporting to camp for his rookie season with the Celtics and edging Magic Johnson for the Rookie of the Year award. In landing Bird, Auerbach made up for his February 1979 trade for Bob McAdoo, when he had dealt three first-round picks for the All-Star, who played just 20 games for the Celtics.

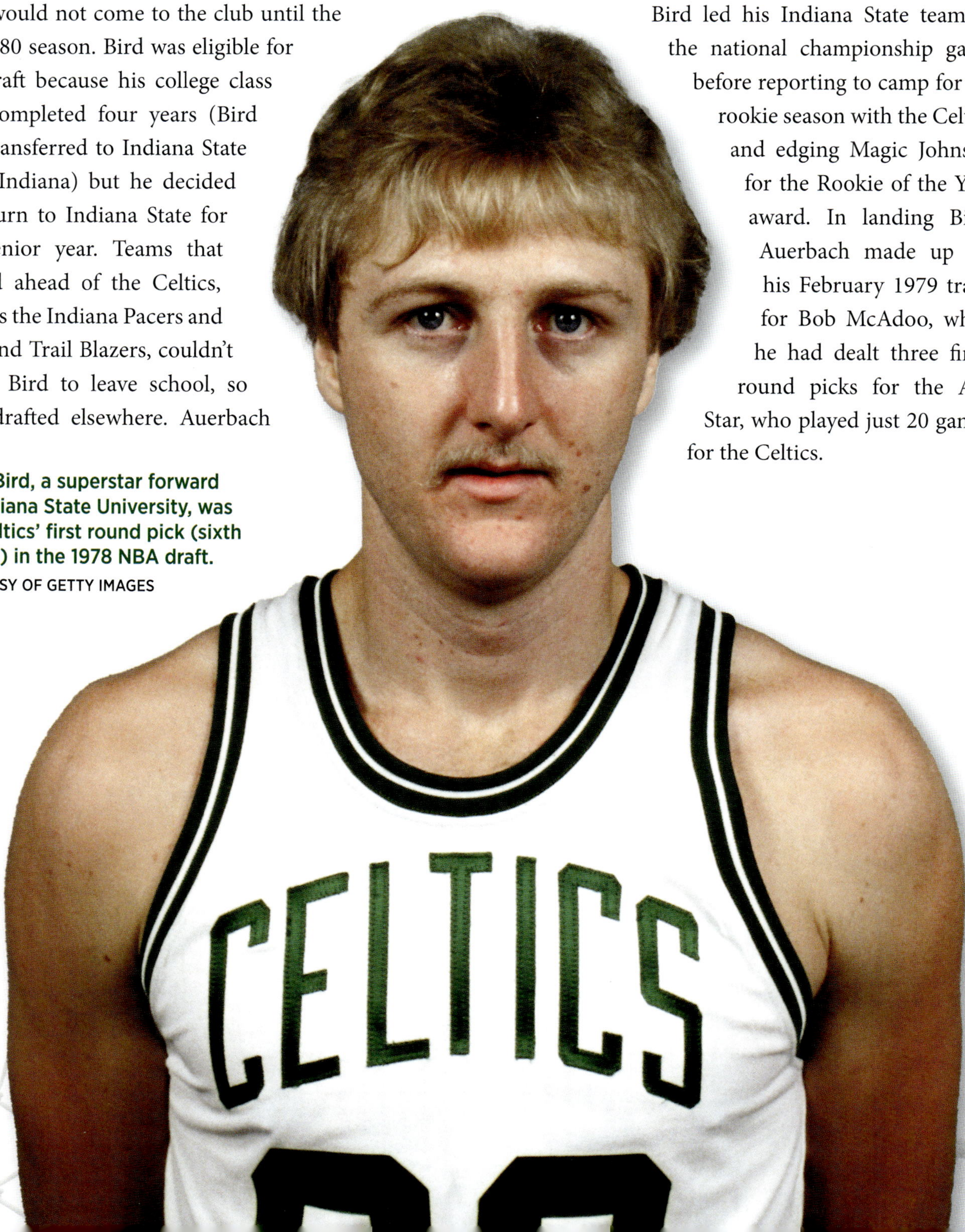

Larry Bird, a superstar forward for Indiana State University, was the Celtics' first round pick (sixth overall) in the 1978 NBA draft.
COURTESY OF GETTY IMAGES

Coach Dave Cowens talks to his team at the Boston Garden, circa 1979.
COURTESY OF GETTY IMAGES

Cowens Becomes the Celtics' Second Player Coach

THE CELTICS FRANCHISE hit some hard times between the 1976 title and the arrival of Larry Bird in 1979. The 1976–77 club was aging and were ousted in the Eastern Conference playoffs by the eventual conference champion Philadelphia 76ers. The 1977–78 season included even more upheaval, with Tom Heinsohn being fired after an 11–23 start and replaced by Satch Sanders. Sanders was fired after a 2–12 start in 1978–79, and he was replaced by veteran center Dave Cowens, who became the second player-coach in team history. Cowens couldn't work miracles with this roster. He finished 27–41 in his coaching stint on a team besieged by injuries that was also aging. Cowens would later become an NBA head coach for the Golden State Warriors and Charlotte Hornets after his playing career. But he returned to just a player role after the 1978–79 season, when the Celtics hired well-traveled Bill Fitch as their head coach. The Celtics would also be boosted by Bird's arrival, and the franchise would return to prosperity a few years later.

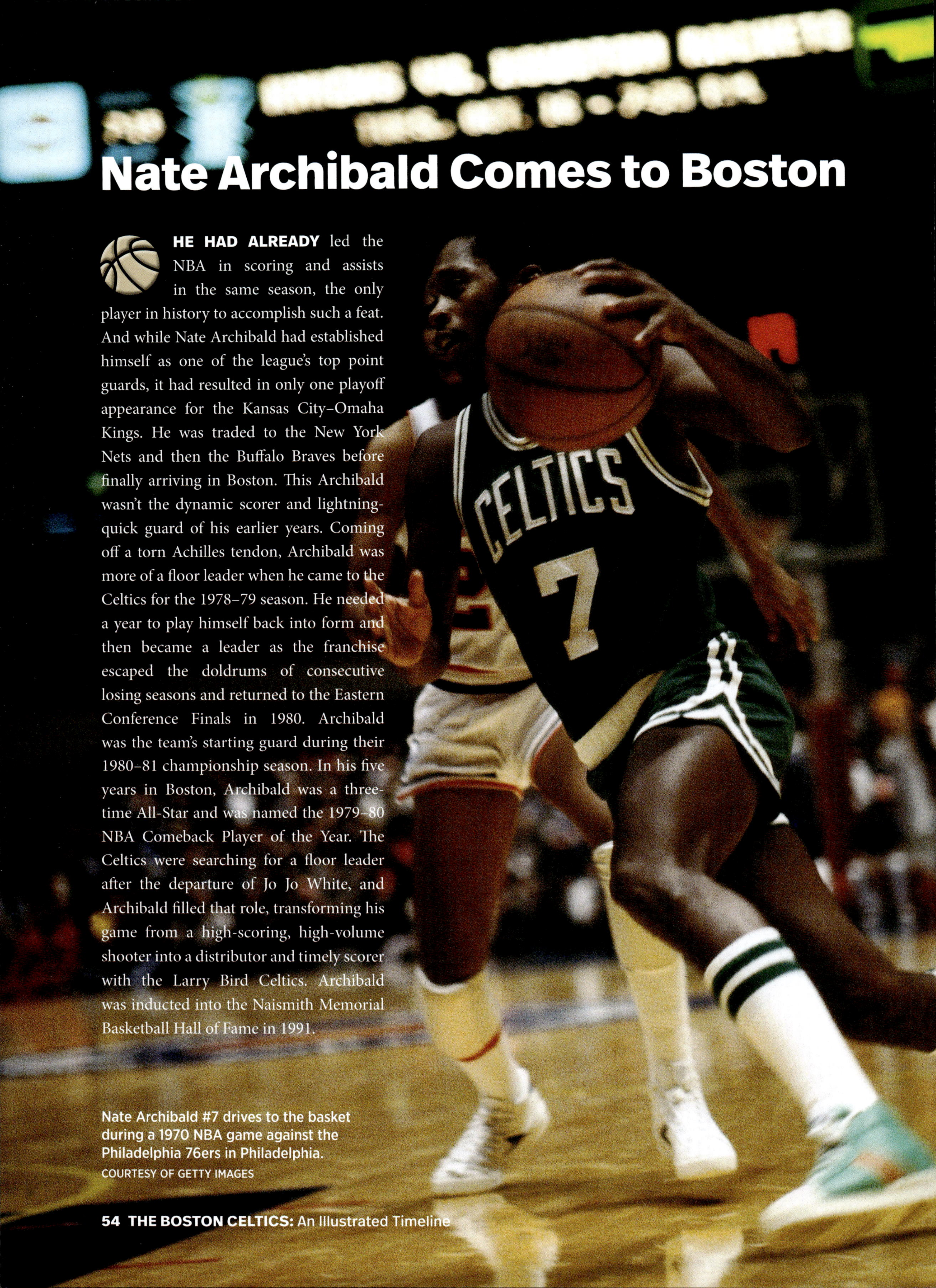

Nate Archibald Comes to Boston

HE HAD ALREADY led the NBA in scoring and assists in the same season, the only player in history to accomplish such a feat. And while Nate Archibald had established himself as one of the league's top point guards, it had resulted in only one playoff appearance for the Kansas City–Omaha Kings. He was traded to the New York Nets and then the Buffalo Braves before finally arriving in Boston. This Archibald wasn't the dynamic scorer and lightning-quick guard of his earlier years. Coming off a torn Achilles tendon, Archibald was more of a floor leader when he came to the Celtics for the 1978–79 season. He needed a year to play himself back into form and then became a leader as the franchise escaped the doldrums of consecutive losing seasons and returned to the Eastern Conference Finals in 1980. Archibald was the team's starting guard during their 1980–81 championship season. In his five years in Boston, Archibald was a three-time All-Star and was named the 1979–80 NBA Comeback Player of the Year. The Celtics were searching for a floor leader after the departure of Jo Jo White, and Archibald filled that role, transforming his game from a high-scoring, high-volume shooter into a distributor and timely scorer with the Larry Bird Celtics. Archibald was inducted into the Naismith Memorial Basketball Hall of Fame in 1991.

Nate Archibald #7 drives to the basket during a 1970 NBA game against the Philadelphia 76ers in Philadelphia.
COURTESY OF GETTY IMAGES

Pete Maravich

PETE MARAVICH IS associated with the Atlanta Hawks and New Orleans Jazz, but the all-time great guard actually finished his career with the Celtics. General Manager Red Auerbach was seeking bench help to aid the 1979–80 club led by Larry Bird, and Maravich had just been waived by the Utah Jazz. After years of dazzling NBA fans with his scoring prowess and passing skills, Maravich was in decline, as knee issues curtailed his career. Still, he joined the Celtics in January of 1980 and played in 26 regular-season games, averaging 11.5 points per game on 49.4 percent shooting, a career best. Maravich also logged his first playoff action in seven years, helping the Celtics to the Eastern Conference Finals. Maravich enjoyed his share of moments, such as a vintage 31-point game against the Indiana Pacers and a 20-point effort two nights later against the Detroit Pistons. Maravich would retire after the 1979–80 season because of recurring knee problems, but he was elected to the Naismith Memorial Basketball Hall of Fame in 1987.

Pete Maravich during a game against the Washington Bullets at Capital Center circa 1980 in Washington, D.C.
COURTESY OF GETTY IMAGES

The NBA's First 3-Pointer

CHRIS FORD ENJOYED a solid 10-year NBA career with the Detroit Pistons and Celtics, and he eventually coached the Celtics in the 1990s. But he will go down in NBA history as the first player to hit a 3-point shot. While the American Basketball Association had adopted the 3-point shot in the late 1960s to make the league more exciting, the NBA didn't adopt the bonus shot until the 1979–80 season. And while the 3-point shot has revolutionized today's game, it was a small part of NBA offenses 40 years ago. On October 12, 1979, on opening night at the Boston Garden for the 1979–80 season, Chris Ford attempted one 3-pointer against the Houston Rockets—and he swished it, becoming the first NBA player to make a 3-pointer in the league's history. Ford would not make another 3-pointer for another 15 games, but he would then go five for seven in a November 28 home win against the Denver Nuggets. Ford would go on to hit 70 3-pointers in that inaugural season, finishing second in the NBA in 3-point percentage while the Celtics were second in the NBA in 3-pointers made.

Chris Ford #42 moves the ball against Mark Olberding #53 of the San Antonio Spurs during a game played in 1979 at the Boston Garden.
COURTESY OF GETTY IMAGES

Bird Wins Rookie of the Year

THE RIVALRY BETWEEN Larry Bird and Earvin "Magic" Johnson dates back to the Michigan State–Indiana State national championship game in 1979, when Johnson's Spartans edged out Bird's Sycamores. But their rivalry continued into the NBA, and Bird won the first round by edging out Johnson for the 1979–80 NBA Rookie of the Year award. Bird was taken in the 1978 draft but returned to Indiana State for his senior season while Johnson was the top pick in the 1979 draft. Both enjoyed stellar rookie seasons, as Johnson led the Los Angeles Lakers to the first championship since 1972 while Bird took a team that won 29 games the previous season to the Eastern Conference Finals. Bird averaged 21.3 points, 10.4 rebounds and 4.5 assists as the Celtics won a league-best 61 games and the Atlantic Division. Johnson averaged 18 points, 7.7 rebounds and 7.3 assists as the Lakers won 60 games and the Pacific Division. While Johnson had considerable help with six-time MVP Kareem Abdul-Jabbar, Norm Nixon, and Jamaal Wilkes, Bird was the Celtics' number one option, playing with an aging Dave Cowens as well as Nate Archibald, Cedric Maxwell, and M.L. Carr. Bird was also third in NBA in 3-point percentage but also finished fourth in MVP voting behind Abdul-Jabbar, Julius Erving, and George Gervin. While Johnson's team won the championship again, Bird got the best of Johnson for the individual award. But Bird would get the team accolades in his second season.

Larry Bird #33 and Julius Erving #6 of the Philadelphia 76ers look up during a game played in 1980 at the Boston Garden.
COURTESY OF GETTY IMAGES

Bill Fitch Named Coach of the Year

BEFORE BILL FITCH was hired as Celtics coach before the 1979–80 season, he was considered a franchise reviver, as he had turned the struggling Cleveland Cavaliers into a playoff team during his nine seasons. But he resigned after the 1978–79 season with another opportunity in mind. Two days after he left Cleveland, Fitch was hired as coach of the Celtics, and he led the once-proud franchise back to respectability behind rookie Larry Bird. The Celtics finished 61-21, their best record since the 1972–73 season. For that mark, Fitch received his first and only NBA Coach of the Year Award. The Celtics had improved by 32 wins from the season before, the biggest one-year improvement in franchise history, and they advanced to the Eastern Conference Finals before losing to the Philadelphia 76ers. Fitch helped blend a team with a young Bird and emerging Cedric Maxwell along with veterans Dave Cowens, Nate Archibald, and Chris Ford. Fitch instilled discipline and structure into an organization that had lost its momentum since the days of Tom Heinsohn. General Manager Red Auerbach's hunch to go after Fitch worked perfectly, as he would lead the Celtics to the NBA championship the next season, But Fitch finally got his long-awaited respect as a head coach by being named Coach of the Year.

Coach Bill Fitch.
COURTESY OF GETTY IMAGES

The Trade that Created a Dynasty: The Celtics-Warriors Deal

RED AUERBACH WAS a shrewd general manager, and he was able to get a return on disgruntled veteran Bob McAdoo, who played just 20 games with the Celtics. He traded McAdoo to the Detroit Pistons for two first-round picks in the 1980 draft. Then Auerbach flipped those two picks for two future cornerstones. Just a day before the draft, Auerbach traded two first rounders, Nos. 1 and 13 overall, to the Golden State Warriors for the third pick and veteran center Robert Parish. The Warriors believed Purdue's Joe Barry Carroll was a franchise player and drafted him with the Celtics' No. 1 pick. The Warriors took center Rickey Brown with the 13th pick. Boston, meanwhile, countered by using the Warriors pick (No. 3) on Minnesota center Kevin McHale. Well . . . McHale and Parish would team with Larry Bird to form the team's Big Three and lead the franchise to three championships, including in the 1980–81 season. Carroll would never meet expectations, and Brown played just two seasons in Golden State. Parish would play 21 NBA seasons, reach nine All-Star Games and win four championships. McHale would play in seven All-Star Games, win three championships, and make six all-defense teams. It was considered one of the most lopsided trades in NBA history. The Celtics grabbed Bird, McHale, and Parish in a two-year span to resurrect their franchise and turn into another powerhouse in the 1980s. This deal was one of the reasons why teams feared consummating trades with Red Auerbach.

Adrian Dantley #4 of the Utah Jazz rebounds against Kevin McHale #32 and Robert Parish #00 in a game played in 1981 at the Boston Garden.
COURTESY OF GETTY IMAGES

The Chief, Robert Parish

WHAT ROBERT PARISH didn't deliver in quotes or outward emotion, he more than made up for with his production over a brilliant stretch with the Celtics. Nicknamed "The Chief," Parish was a defensive stalwart in the paint with the ability to score at the rim or with the short jumper. In 14 seasons with the Celtics—which included three championships and two other NBA Finals appearances—Parish averaged 16.5 points and 10 rebounds per game. He accepted a complimentary offensive role, with Kevin McHale and Larry Bird taking lead roles, and he shined consistently, reaching nine All-Star Games. Parish also was the most reliable and durable player in league history, setting the mark for games played with 1,611. In all, he logged 21 NBA seasons, winning a championship in 1997 with Michael Jordan and the Chicago Bulls. Parish, who is second all-time in Celtics games played behind John Havlicek, continued the Celtics' great tradition of centers that had included Bill Russell and Dave Cowens and went on with players such as Kevin Garnett. Parish, second all-time in rebounding behind Russell, had his No. 00 retired by the Celtics on January 18, 1998. He was named to the NBA's 50th and 75th anniversary teams and inducted into the Naismith Basketball Hall of Fame in 2003.

Robert Parish poses for a portrait circa 1981 at the Boston Garden.
COURTESY OF GETTY IMAGES

Game 7 of the 1981 Eastern Conference Finals

THE CELTICS RECONNECTED with the defending Eastern Conference champion Philadelphia 76ers in the 1981 Eastern Finals. This time the Celtics had Robert Parish and Kevin McHale on their roster, but the 76ers didn't appear daunted. Behind Julius Erving, the 76ers won three of the first four games, with two of their three series wins coming by three points. The Celtics would bounce back to even the series with two two-point wins, leading up to the epic Game 7 at Boston Garden. The two teams went back and forth, but the 76ers took a seven-point lead before Larry Bird led a Celtics comeback. Boston scratched its way to a tie before Bird hit a difficult 18-foot bank shot off the fast break to give the Celtics a 91–89 lead. With 34 seconds left, Philadelphia's Maurice Cheeks was fouled on a drive to the basket and had a chance to tie the game but missed the first free throw. The Celtics responded by working the clock down to five seconds before M.L. Carr missed a jump shot, but Robert Parish knocked the rebound away to kill more time, and the 76ers had just one second left to get off the winning shot. Bobby Jones's inbounds pass hit the top of the backboard, and the Celtics fans stormed the court, as Boston returned to the NBA Finals for the first time in five years. Bird and Erving each finished with 23 points, but the key contributor was forward Cedric Maxwell, who scored 19 points on 9-for-12 shooting.

Outstretched arms reach for Larry Bird (center, #33) as he leaves the basketball court for the dressing room after the Celtics defeated the 76ers, 91–90, to win the seventh and deciding game of the NBA's Eastern Conference title.
COURTESY OF GETTY IMAGES

Former Indiana Univeristy star Landon Turner and head coach of Indiana Hoosiers men's basketball, Mike Woodson, attend a 2023 Coach Woodson Indianapolis event.
COURTESY OF GETTY IMAGES

Celtics Draft Indiana Center Landon Turner

LANDON TURNER WAS the starting center on the 1981 Indiana University basketball team that won the NCAA championship. Just a few months after helping the Hoosiers win the title, he was involved in a tragic car accident that left him paralyzed from the waist down. Turner was entering his senior season and was expected to be a cornerstone for Indiana as well as an NBA prospect. Indiana coach Bobby Knight suggested to friend Red Auerbach that the Celtics draft Turner as a kind gesture. Auerbach obliged. With the 225th and final pick in the 1982 NBA Draft, the Celtics selected Turner. Turner actually reached out to Auerbach and jokingly asked when the club wanted him to report to training camp. It was one of the many gestures of kindness by Auerbach, who went a step further. According to Turner, Auerbach sent him commemorative watches after the 1984 and 1986 Celtics championships. Turner would eventually earn his degree from Indiana after his accident.

Celtics Acquire Dennis Johnson

AFTER HAVING GREAT success with a former high-scoring guard as a floor leader, the Celtics decided to try their luck again with Dennis Johnson. With Nate Archibald, who helped the Celtics to the 1981 title, reaching his 30s, team president Red Auerbach took a chance on Johnson, known as a staunch defender with a surly demeanor. Auerbach had faith that Johnson could become a team leader and also help defend against Philadelphia's Andrew Toney, who had scorched the Celtics' defense in their playoff meetings in 1981 and 1982. Johnson came to Boston in another brilliant Auerbach trade, with the Celtics giving the Phoenix Suns backup center Rick Robey and two second-round picks. Johnson left all of his issues back in Phoenix, turning into that dependable point guard and solid defender the Celtics sought. He was the primary defender against Magic Johnson in those epic NBA Finals matchups with the Los Angeles Lakers, and he was the point guard who got McHale, Parish, Bird, and Danny Ainge into the right spots. He was also the player who made that difficult back-handed layup after Bird stole the ball from Isiah Thomas in that stunning Game 5 comeback in 1987 against the Detroit Pistons. "DJ" was the glue who held those 1984 and 1986 title teams together, the perfect addition to a championship-caliber team. Johnson played his final seven seasons with the Celtics before retiring in 1990. Johnson's No. 3 was retired on December 13, 1991. Johnson passed away in 2007 at age 52.

Dennis Johnson looks on during a game played at Madison Square Garden in 1989.
COURTESY OF GETTY IMAGES

The Mastery of Kevin McHale

HIS FOOTWORK WAS masterful, and he had a soft, feathery touch around the basket. Kevin McHale was one of the best power forwards in NBA history, a brilliant all-around player who was at the nucleus of those 1980s Celtics teams, partnering with Larry Bird, Robert Parish, Cedric Maxwell, and Dennis Johnson for those great title runs. Celtics president Red Auerbach acquired the third overall pick a day before the 1980 draft, along with Golden State center Robert Parish, and then selected McHale, the University of Minnesota standout. McHale immediately became a reliable reserve for coach Bill Fitch, and he came off the bench for most of the first five years before being a staple in the starting lineup. McHale was a seven-time All-Star, was a two-time Sixth Man of the Year, and was named to the NBA's 50th anniversary and 75th anniversary teams. He helped revolutionize the game for post players, using his footwork to score from midrange and at the rim. His best season was 1986–87, when he averaged 26.1 points per game and led the NBA with 60.4 percent shooting from the field. He also set the Celtics' record with 56 points during a 138–129 win over the Detroit Pistons on March 3, 1985. That record would last only a few days before his buddy Bird scored 60 on the Atlanta Hawks. McHale was elected to the Naismith Memorial Basketball Hall of Fame in 1999 and eventually became a successful head coach and general manager for his hometown Minnesota Timberwolves.

Kevin McHale poses for a portrait circa 1981 at the Boston Garden.
COURTESY OF GETTY IMAGES

Celtics Return to the Top Behind Young Larry Bird

THE 1980–81 CELTICS were primed for a deep playoff run. Red Auerbach had acquired center Robert Parish and drafted power forward Kevin McHale to go along with a second-year Larry Bird, who was determined to avenge the conference final loss to the Philadelphia 76ers the prior year. The Celtics tied the 76ers with 62 wins in the Atlantic Division and easily took care of the Chicago Bulls in the first round of the playoffs. The Celtics then met Philadelphia, but the 76ers jumped out to a three-games-to-one lead, with two of those wins by a combined three points. In typical Celtics tradition, Boston rallied, taking Games 5 and 6 each by two-point margins and then using a running Bird jumper to edge Philadelphia 91–90 in an amazing Game 7 win. The Celtics were awaiting the Lakers, but that didn't happen. Los Angeles spent the season in chaos with a coaching change and Magic Johnson trade demand, and it lost to the Houston Rockets in the first round of the playoffs. The Rockets then knocked off the Spurs and Kings to reach the Finals. The Celtics could do little to stop the great Moses Malone through the first four games, and the teams were tied at 2–2 heading into Game 5 at the Garden. Cedric Maxwell turned in a brilliant performance with 28 points and 15 rebounds as Boston ran away 109–80. In Game 6, all five starters scored in double figures and Tiny Archibald dished out 12 assists in a 102–91 win. It was the first championship for Bird and the rest of the Big Three, and the beginning of a dynasty.

Larry Bird holds the championship trophy over his head during the Celtics' 1981 Championship parade in Boston.
COURTESY OF GETTY IMAGES

Celtics fans cheer during a game played in 1982 at the Boston Garden.
COURTESY OF GETTY IMAGES

Losing to the 76ers in 1982: "Beat LA!"

THE 1982 CELTICS once again raced to the best record in the Eastern Conference, winning 63 games and looking primed to return to the NBA Finals for a second consecutive season. But they ran into the Philadelphia 76ers in the Eastern Conference Finals and a 76ers guard named Andrew Toney. Nicknamed the "Boston Strangler" for his stellar games against the Celtics, Toney averaged 22.1 points in the thrilling seven-game series against Boston. The Celtics fell behind three games to one but rallied to tie the series and hosted the deciding game. But unlike so many Game 7s where the Celtics figured ways to pull out last-minute wins this crew was exhausted and Philadelphia pulled away. When the 76ers had sealed the game and Boston coach Bill Fitch finally decided to pull his starters, the Boston Garden crowd began a chant. The fans started screaming, "Beat LA!" as an encouragement to the 76ers to beat the rival Lakers in the NBA Finals. The Celtics players such as M.L. Carr said they had more respect for the 76ers because of their rugged battles during the regular season and playoffs, and the Celtics fans decided to take sides with Philadelphia facing the Lakers for the second time in three years. The "Beat LA!" chant became famous, with every Los Angeles sports rival using it to cheer against the Dodgers, Lakers, Clippers, Sparks, and even the Rams. But it was most notably used against the Lakers for the next 40 years.

Cowens Returns to Boston—with the Milwaukee Bucks

DAVE COWENS'S CELTICS journey was definitely an unusual one. After being the fourth overall pick in 1970 and helping the club to titles in 1974 and 1976, things became bizarre in Boston. Cowens took a personal leave of absence in 1976 because of undisclosed issues, including an apparent problem with coach Tom Heinsohn. After Heinsohn was eventually fired (as was his replacement, Satch Sanders), Cowens became the Celtics' second player-coach, finishing the 1978–79 season in that role. Cowens eventually retired during the 1980 preseason, missing a chance for a third title with Boston. Eventually, however, at age 34, Cowens decided he wanted to make a comeback. However, by then the Celtics were already set in the frontcourt with Larry Bird, Kevin McHale, and Robert Parish, so Cowens asked the club to trade his rights to another contender. Red Auerbach traded the retired Cowens to the Milwaukee Bucks on September 9, 1982, for guard Quinn Buckner. Cowens played 40 games for the Bucks in that season, including a return to Boston Garden on October 14, 1982 for a preseason game. Cowens received a three-minute standing ovation, according to the *New York Times*, and helped his team to a win. He was back in Boston a month later for a regular season game. Wearing No. 36, Cowens scored 10 points with nine rebounds in 25 minutes as the Bucks won again, 105–101. A crowd of 15,320 at the Garden gave Cowens another ovation. Cowens was injured in the regular-season's final game and did not get a chance to play in the first-round series with the Celtics. He retired after his lone season with the Bucks.

Dave Cowens of the Milwaukee Bucks poses for a portrait circa 1982 at the MECCA in Milwaukee, Wisconsin.

COURTESY OF GETTY IMAGES

K.C. Jones Takes Over for Bill Fitch

THE CELTICS WERE in a decline after winning the title in 1981. They were eliminated by the Philadelphia 76ers in seven games in '82, and then the '83 club was swept in the second round by the Milwaukee Bucks. It was time for a change. Larry Bird appeared discontent with the coaching style of Bill Fitch despite his early success in Boston. Fitch surprisingly resigned four weeks after the Bucks series, and Auerbach replaced him with a familiar face: assistant coach K.C. Jones, an all-time great Celtic who won eight championships in his nine seasons in Boston. Jones had been a head coach previously, leading the Washington Bullets past the Celtics and into the NBA Finals in 1975, and he joined the Celtics staff in 1977. The Celtics players needed a new voice, and the quiet but no-nonsense Jones was the right decision. Jones led the Celtics to NBA titles in 1984 and 1986, using his basketball acumen, defensive knowledge, and calm demeanor to take the Celtics to the next level. He coached five seasons for the Celtics, leading Boston to the NBA Finals in four of those seasons, before stepping down after the 1987–88 season.

Head coach K.C. Jones looks on from the sidelines during an NBA game circa 1983–88 at the Boston Garden.
COURTESY OF GETTY IMAGES

Players rejoice on the Celtics bench during Game Seven of the NBA Finals between the Celtics and the Los Angeles Lakers at the Boston Garden on June 12, 1984.
COURTESY OF GETTY IMAGES

Celtics Return to the Top, Beat Magic & Lakers in '84

UNDER FIRST-YEAR COACH K.C. Jones, the Celtics were on a mission in 1983–84, winning a league-best 62 games behind MVP Larry Bird along with Robert Parish, Kevin McHale, Danny Ainge, and Cedric Maxwell. They rolled into the playoffs, beating the Washington Bullets in the first round and edging the New York Knicks in seven games before beating the Milwaukee Bucks in the Eastern Conference Finals. The NBA Finals opponent was a familiar one in the Los Angeles Lakers, but it was the teams' first meeting in the finals in 15 years. In an emotional and physical series, the Lakers appeared to be in control with their up-tempo style until Kevin McHale's hard foul on Kurt Rambis almost incited a brawl. The Celtics used their physicality to take control of the series. The Lakers had a chance to take the first two games in Boston before James Worthy's errant pass late in Game 2 was stolen by Gerald Henderson, helping the Celtics to an eventual overtime win. The Lakers staved off elimination in Game 6 in Los Angeles, bringing the series back to Boston Garden for another epic Game 7. In a sweltering Garden, the Celtics outhustled and outmanned the Lakers in that deciding game, taking control in the third quarter behind the brilliance of series MVP Bird, who exacted revenge on rival Magic Johnson in their first finals matchup since their NCAA championship meeting five years earlier. Johnson averaged 18 points and 13 assists but made some key mistakes during the series, earning him the nickname "Tragic Johnson" from Boston fans.

Larry Bird, Master of the Triple-Double

BEFORE TRIPLE-DOUBLES became popular, before Russell Westbrook, LeBron James, and Jason Kidd were racking them up, Larry Bird filled up the boxscores with his versatility. He finished with 59 career triple-doubles, a franchise record. What people tend to ignore about Bird is that he averaged a double-double (24.3 points and 10 rebounds), in addition to 6.3 assists, over his career. Bird's career high in points was 60, in rebounds it was 21, and in assists it was 17. Bird's best year for versatility may have been 1984–85, when he collected eight triple-doubles, including one on March 5, 1985, at New York, when he scored 20 points with 19 rebounds and 10 assists in a 110-102 win over the Knicks. In his MVP season of 1985–86 Bird amassed 10 triple-doubles, his best game being a 15-point win at Golden State when he scored 36 points along with 12 rebounds and 11 assists. Bird was known for winning along with his remarkable passing ability and court savvy as well as his pure jump shot. But he was a better rebounder than given credit for, and he is considered one of the best all-around players in league history.

Larry Bird #33 shoots against Julius Erving #6 of the Philadelphia 76ers circa 1985 at the Spectrum in Philadelphia.
COURTESY OF GETTY IMAGES

Larry Bird #33 boxes out against Mark Eaton #53 of the Utah Jazz during a game played in 1985 at the Boston Garden.
COURTESY OF GETTY IMAGES

Larry Bird Sets Club Record with Nine Steals

IN ONE OF the more masterful performances of his career, Larry Bird was one steal from a quadruple double in a 110–94 win over the Utah Jazz on February 18, 1985. Bird, in his prime and in the midst of three consecutive MVP awards, was brilliant in all facets of the game. He collected a triple-double that night with 30 points, 12 rebounds, 10 assists, and a club record nine steals. What's even more astounding about the Bird feat was that he accomplished those numbers in just 33 minutes as the Celtics put the Jazz away early. Bird was an underrated defender, and his basketball instincts allowed him to read passing lanes for steals. In addition to being named All-NBA 10 times, Bird was named second-team All-Defense three times, a little-known fact. Bird remains 40th all-time in steals in NBA history with 1,556 and eighth in postseason steals with 296.

Getting the Big Redhead

AFTER THE 1984–1985 season, Red Auerbach asked Larry Bird what the Celtics needed to return to championship level after losing in the NBA Finals to the rival Los Angeles Lakers. Bird said the team needed more toughness in the paint, more focus from the beginning of the season to the end, and more leadership. Auerbach responded with a controversial deal, trading 1981 NBA Finals MVP Cedric Maxwell to the Los Angeles Clippers for aging and oft-injured Bill Walton. A knee injury had limited Maxwell to 57 games in 1984–85. Coach K.C. Jones had replaced Maxwell with Kevin McHale in the starting lineup, and Maxwell's impact declined. Walton stepped in and accepted the backup center role in 1985–86, sparking a franchise that needed grit, hunger and leadership. Walton was nine years removed from his previous NBA championship in 1977, and he was nearing the end of his career. Walton provided a spark, playing well when he was on the floor and proving durable despite his injury-plagued past. Walton knew he wasn't the player of the 1970s when he was a dominant cornerstone with the Portland Trail Blazers. And he blended in well with Bird, McHale, Parish, and the rest of the cast, helping the Celtics win another championship and capping his career on top. Because of foot issues, Walton would play just 10 more games with the Celtics the following year before retiring. He was named to the NBA's 50th and 75th Anniversary teams and also the Naismith Memorial Basketball Hall of Fame. He passed away in 2024.

Bill Walton during a game at the Omni in Atlanta, circa 1990.
COURTESY OF GETTY IMAGES

Celtics Win Three Consecutive Sixth Man of the Year Awards

BEFORE THE SIXTH Man of the Year became an official award in 1982–83, the Celtics valued the role of the first player off the bench. For more than a decade John Havlicek, and Frank Ramsey before him, mastered the reserve role, playing starter's minutes, finishing games, and being one of the best players on the floor. Havlicek didn't receive any honors for this because he played far before the award was implemented. Yet Kevin McHale and Bill Walton were fortunate enough to benefit. McHale, one of greatest power forwards of all time, was the first multiple Sixth Man of the Year Award winner, taking the honor in 1983–84 and 1984–85 with impressive numbers (18.4 points and 7.4 rebounds in the first year and 19.8/9.0 in the second). Walton then took home the award when McHale was moved to the starting lineup in 1985–86. Often injured during his career, Walton was acquired by the Celtics from the Los Angeles Clippers as a career revival. Walton was able to stay remarkably healthy, playing in 80 games. And while his numbers weren't eye popping, Walton became a reliable backup center, averaging 7.6 points and 6.8 rebounds in helping the Celtics to their third championship in five years. Walton proved he could stay on the floor and be a productive player after years of foot issues had prevented him from reaching his potential following a stellar start to his career.

Bill Walton #5 shoots over Kareem Abdul-Jabbar #33 of the Los Angeles Lakers during a game in 1985 at The Forum in Inglewood, California.
COURTESY OF GETTY IMAGES

Jordan Scores 63 at Boston Garden, but Celtics Win

PERHAPS IT WAS the day the legend began. The Celtics were on their way to another championship in 1986 but had to face an upstart Chicago Bulls team led by a rising star named Michael Jordan in the first round of the NBA playoffs. The Celtics were by far the more talented team, but Jordan was the best player in the series, displaying his dazzling skills on the playoff stage for just the second time. After the Celtics fought off Jordan and the Bulls despite his 49 points in Game 1, they hosted Game 2 at Boston Garden, likely thinking they had already withstood Jordan's best punch. Not quite. Game 2 of the series was a Jordan showcase, one of the finest individual playoff performances in league history, as Jordan set the record for the most points ever in a postseason game. The Celtics and Bulls traded blows, with Jordan and Orlando Woolridge making up the majority of the Chicago offense. Boston had to rally in the fourth quarter to send the game into overtime. Jordan singlehandedly battled the Celtics into double overtime, scoring 63 points on 22-for-41 shooting and going 19 for 21 from the free throw line. The Bulls didn't have enough help for Jordan to win the series, or even a game, but Jordan walked away impressing the Celtics and the basketball world. The Celtics got the sweep, but Jordan averaged 43.7 points with 50 percent shooting. A star was born.

Michael Jordan of the Chicago Bulls shoots over Danny Ainge #44 during Game One of the Eastern Conference Quarterfinals played on April 17, 1986 at the Boston Garden. The Celtics won 123–104.

COURTESY OF GETTY IMAGES

Death of Len Bias

HOW DID THE Celtics get the No. 2 pick after winning the NBA Finals in 1986? They had traded Gerald Henderson to the Seattle SuperSonics after the 1984 season for their pick. Red Auerbach had his sights set on a young, athletic Maryland forward named Len Bias, who embraced and relished playing in Boston. The Celtics took Bias, who was thrilled with the opportunity to play for the defending champions. Then, in one of the more heartbreaking stories in sports history, Bias collapsed in a dorm room at the University of Maryland two days after the 1986 NBA Draft. Bias was apparently using cocaine with friends and teammates and passed away of cardiac arrest. Bias, an All-American and gifted player, was supposed to take the reins of the Celtics from Larry Bird, Kevin McHale, and Robert Parish. He was considered the future of the franchise, and the Celtics and NBA world were robbed of witnessing his brilliance on the floor. A distraught Auerbach presented Bias's No. 30 to his parents. Bias told reporters during his trip to Boston following the draft how excited he was about wearing the green uniform and helping the Celtics win another championship. The loss of Bias would impact the Celtics franchise for decades, and it sparked a change in attitudes about drug use and addiction across the country.

Number one draft pick Len Bias of the Celtics pumps his fist after he was selected second overall in the June 1986 NBA draft.
COURTESY OF GETTY IMAGES

McHale Scores a Celtics Best 56 Points

KEVIN MCHALE HAD nights when he was the best player on the floor. There were nights where he couldn't be stopped in the post, where his jump shot swished again and again. One of those nights was March 3, 1985, when the Celtics hosted the Detroit Pistons at Boston Garden. Against a team that would eventually become one of their primary rivals in the Eastern Conference, McHale scored a career-high and Celtics-best 56 points in a 138–129 win. McHale was 22-for-28 shooting and 12 for 13 from the free throw line, and he added 16 rebounds and 3 blocks in a magnificent performance. McHale broke Larry Bird's previous franchise record of 53 points when Bird threw a long inbounds pass to McHale for a bank shot. K.C. Jones removed McHale after his scored his 56 to a standing ovation on an amazing night. McHale also added 10 offensive rebounds—he scored a handful of buckets on putbacks—and the Celtics had an incredible 159 offensive rating (points per 100 possessions) when he was on the floor. While Bird delivered the assist that gave McHale the record, he would duly note that McHale set the club record. In Larry Bird fashion, he eclipsed McHale's 56-point outing with 60 just nine days later against the Atlanta Hawks in New Orleans.

Kevin McHale reacts after scoring 56 points during a game against the Detroit Pistons at the Boston Garden, March 3, 1985.
COURTESY OF GETTY IMAGES

Bird Drops 60 in the Big Easy

THE ATLANTA HAWKS used to play a handful of home games in New Orleans after the Jazz moved to Utah, and when they hosted the Celtics in the Big Easy on March 12, 1985, they witnessed the most masterful scoring performance ever by a Boston player. Nine days after Kevin McHale set the franchise record with 56 points, Larry Bird sought to top his buddy and frontcourt teammate. Bird had been responsible for the assist that helped McHale break Bird's own 53-point record. He would reclaim that record with a brilliant display of shooting so impressive that even the Hawks bench players were cheering after buckets. Amazingly, despite Bird being a 3-point specialist in those days, he made just one 3-pointer that night. He went to work on the Hawks from the midrange, hitting an array of leaning jumpers. In a few second-half sequences, Bird made tough jumpers near the Hawks bench, sending the bench players into a frenzy with awe. In 43 minutes, Bird went 22 for 36 from the field and hit 15-of-16 free throws. He was at his masterful best, chewing up any defender in his path, most notably Naismith Basketball Hall of Famer Dominique Wilkins. In the final seconds of the third quarter, Bird dribbled the ball toward Atlanta center Rickey Brown and launched a beautiful floater that beat the buzzer. With the fans at Lakefront Arena on their feet in delight, Bird ended his barrage with a jumper at the buzzer for 60 points.

Larry Bird #33 shoots against the Atlanta Hawks during a game played circa 1990 at the Omni in Atlanta, Georgia.
COURTESY OF GETTY IMAGES

Almost Perfect at Home in '86

THE 1985–86 CELTICS were a machine, determined to recapture the championship after losing to the Los Angeles Lakers in 1985. And no other Celtics team has ever been better at the Boston Garden. The 1985–86 Celtics were a stellar 40–1 at home that season, their lone loss being to the Portland Trail Blazers on December 6, 1985, when Larry Bird missed 17 of 26 shots. The Celtics went on to win their next 31 home games and then went 10–0 in the playoffs for a combined 50–1 home record. Perhaps it was the parquet floor or those Garden rims, but the Celtics were statistically better at the Garden than on the road. They scored 8.3 more points at home than away from Boston, they outscored opponents by 13 points per game, and they collected seven more assists per game. In addition, the Celtics only scored fewer than 100 points at home once, a 94–88 win over the New York Knicks, and they bested the Lakers in an NBA Finals rematch with an easy 110–95 win. Boston Garden was one of the toughest places to play in the NBA, and the 1985–86 Celtics proved that with their near flawless record.

Dennis Johnson #3 moves the ball against John Paxson of the Portland Trailblazers during a game played in 1986 at the Boston Garden.
COURTESY OF GETTY IMAGES

Larry Bird Wins Three Consecutive MVPs

LARRY BIRD WASN'T the highest jumper or the most imposing player on the basketball floor, but he was one of the best of all time, evidenced by winning three consecutive MVP Awards during his prime in the mid-1980s. While Bird competed with Magic Johnson for NBA championships, he proved to be the best individual player in the league with three magnificent seasons from 1983 to 1986. Bird averaged 24.2 points and 10.1 rebounds per game for his first award in 1983–84, in leading the Celtics to a second NBA championship in four years. He returned in 1984–85 to average 28.7 points and 10.5 rebounds to become the first Celtic since Bill Russell to win consecutive MVP Awards. The following year he cemented his status as a Hall of Famer and all-time great Celtic by matching Russell with three consecutive MVPs when he averaged 25.8 points and 9.8 rebounds, again taking the Celtics to a championship. Bird mastered the midrange jump shot, he became a strong 3-point shooter, and he was also a brilliant passer and quality rebounder. What Bird lacked in pure athleticism he made up for in skill and desire. His three-year stretch in the mid-1980s was perhaps the best basketball ever played by a Celtics player, and Bird emerged as one of the great small forwards of all time. Bird's most prolific season may have occurred in 1987–88 when he averaged a Celtics' record 29.9 points per game, but he finished second in MVP voting to Chicago Bulls guard Michael Jordan, who averaged 35 points per game.

Larry Bird is awarded the trophy for Most Valuable Player, an honor voted on by the New England press, before a game circa 1984 at the Boston Garden.

COURTESY OF GETTY IMAGES

Who's Gonna Finish Second: Larry Bird Wins Three Consecutive 3-Point Contests

LARRY BIRD ALWAYS considered himself the best shooter in the world during his playing days, and the 1986 All-Star Weekend in Dallas was his opportunity to prove it. For the NBA's first ever All-Star Weekend, Bird put on a show in the Long Distance Shootout. Wearing his All-Star uniform, Bird squeaked into the semifinals with the lowest score of all the qualifiers. He got better as the contest progressed, advancing to the final with a top score of 18, earning a meeting with Milwaukee sharpshooter Craig Hodges. After Hodges scored just 12 in the final round, Bird responded with a 3-point showcase, swishing jumper after jumper, including banking in the bonus ball of his fourth rack. He finished with a score of 22, making him the first winner of the 3-Point Contest. In 1987 in Seattle, Bird would go on to edge Dallas's Detlef Schrempf for his second consecutive title. And in what would be a brilliant swan song in Chicago, rumor has it that when Bird walked into the locker room he asked the other seven participants, "OK, so who's going to finish second?"

Bird faced Seattle's Dale Ellis in the Final. Needing to swish the final bonus ball for the victory, Bird raised his arm with his index finger in the air as the ball nestled through the hoop. Bird indeed was the best shooter in the world for three consecutive years. Bird and Hodges were the only three-time winners of the 3-Point Contest, which has become a staple at All-Star Weekend.

Larry Bird holds up his trophy after winning the 3-Point Contest at Reunion Arena in Dallas, Texas, February 8, 1986.
COURTESY OF GETTY IMAGES

Bird to Johnson: The Steal that Stole the Series

Dennis Johnson and Larry Bird raise their hands in victory after Bird stole the ball, passing to Johnson, who scored the winning basket against the Detroit Pistons at the Boston Garden on May 26, 1987.
COURTESY OF GETTY IMAGES

THE BOSTON CELTICS were fully aware the Detroit Pistons were coming. Detroit gradually improved as the 1980s progressed. The Pistons featured Isiah Thomas, a young Dennis Rodman, John Salley, Bill Laimbeer, and Rick Mahorn. The Pistons' stars were reaching their primes while the Celtics were aging. The two teams met in the 1987 Eastern Conference Finals, which would be the last Eastern Conference Finals victory for the Big Three. The Celtics were on the verge of falling behind three games to two with Game 6 headed for Detroit. Down 107–106, Larry Bird darted for the hoop with under 10 seconds left and Rodman blocked the shot, with the ball going off Jerry Sichting's hands with 5 seconds left. Thomas tried to inbound the ball before Boston's defense was set. Fortunately for the Celtics, he lobbed a pass toward Laimbeer that was intercepted by Bird, who, while falling out of bounds, fed the cutting Dennis Johnson for a difficult backhanded layup with one second left. Instead of arguing for a foul call, Bird rose after the blocked layup and broke toward the ball as Thomas released the pass. The moment he saw Bird steal the ball, Johnson raced toward the basket and Bird met him with a perfect pass to set up the layup. It was the type of play champions make in the clutch, and it saved the series for the Celtics. Boston would lose Game 6 at Detroit and then come back home to take the deciding game 117–114 behind 37 points from Bird. It was the last great stand for the Big Three dynasty.

Celtics Draft Local Product Reggie Lewis

THE CELTICS WERE looking to inject their roster with young talent in preparation for life after Larry Bird, Kevin McHale, and Robert Parish. Boston was excited about the potential of 1986 first-round pick Len Bias, but his tragic death shook the organization. Team president Red Auerbach then selected a local kid, Northeastern University forward Reggie Lewis, with Boston's first-round pick in 1987. Luckily for the Celtics, several teams had passed on Lewis and he fell to 22nd—the second-to-last pick of the first round. Lewis had taken Northeastern to the NCAA Tournament, enjoying a sparkling career at the university just 10 minutes from Boston Garden. Lewis was the type of hard-working, humble, and gifted player the Celtics desperately needed to continue their winning tradition. His then-girlfriend Donna Harris told *The Boston Globe* that Lewis shopped for his suit for his Celtics introductory press conference at Filene's Basement, a local department store, and he took a Boston subway to the Garden to meet with the media. Lewis played six seasons for the Celtics, averaging 17.6 points before his tragic death because of heart-related issues in July 1993.

Reggie Lewis #35 defends Michael Jordan #23 of the Chicago Bulls during a game played at the Boston Garden.
COURTESY OF GETTY IMAGES

Bird Outduels Dominique Wilkins in Epic Game 7

AS THE CELTICS dynasty was coming to its conclusion, one of the younger teams in the Eastern Conference that sought to unseat them was the Atlanta Hawks, who pushed the Celtics to the brink in the 1988 Eastern Conference semifinals. Each team defended home court in the first four games before the Hawks won Game 5 in Boston. Then the Celtics stole Game 6 at the Omni, setting up one of the most entertaining Game 7 duels in league history. After Larry Bird guaranteed a Game 7 win, he and Atlanta's Dominique Wilkins exchanged baskets in the final period, with Bird hitting an improbable left-handed hook shot as he was fouled by Cliff Levingston. While the remaining eight players on the floor and both benches watched in awe, Bird and Wilkins exchanged buckets, splashing jumpers regardless of the defense. With the Celtics ahead three points in the final 30 seconds and the Hawks desperately needing a defensive stop, Bird spun around Wilkins and flipped in a nifty left-handed layup. Bird scored 20 points in that fourth quarter on 9-for-10 shooting while Wilkins finished with 47 points on 19-for-33 shooting. In the final sequence, Wilkins dribbled the ball up the floor with the Hawks down 3 in the final seconds. He was intentionally fouled by Danny Ainge to prevent a 3-point attempt. Wilkins intentionally missed the second free throw, but Robert Parish snared the rebound to seal another Game 7 Celtics' victory.

Larry Bird #33 holds ball under his arm as he calls play while being guarded by Hawks' Dominque Wilkins during the first quarter of playoff game at the Boston Garden.
COURTESY OF GETTY IMAGES

Dennis Johnson #3 drives to the basket against the Detroit Pistons in Detroit.
COURTESY OF GETTY IMAGES

The Run is Over: Losing to the Pistons in 1988

IT REQUIRED MAJOR heroics for the Celtics to get past the Detroit Pistons in 1987—that steal by Larry Bird and layup by Dennis Johnson saved them from falling behind three games to two, and they eked out a Game 7 win. But the Pistons weren't going anywhere, and the Celtics were beginning to show signs of age. The Celtics finished the 1987–88 season with the best record in the Eastern Conference and appeared headed for another match with the Los Angeles Lakers in the NBA Finals. But the Eastern Conference Finals began with a Pistons win at Boston Garden as Isiah Thomas scored 35 points. Boston fought back to even the series at 2–2, with a one-point win at the Pontiac Silverdome in Game 4. But the Celtics were running out of gas, and K.C. Jones relied heavily on his starters. In the 102–96 overtime loss to the Pistons in Game 5, just two points came from the bench. What's more, in the six-game series, the Boston bench scored just 58 of the team's 574 points. Bird, Robert Parish, Kevin McHale, and Johnson were aging, and with no bench support, they fell short against the younger, hungrier, and more athletic Pistons. As a sign of respect, when the Celtics walked off the floor following their Game 6 loss at Detroit, McHale pulled aside Thomas and told him and his teammates to go win it all and beat the Lakers. It was the end of the Celtics' dynasty.

The Johnny Most Era

THE RASPY VOICE, perhaps partially created by chain smoking, was legendary in Boston and throughout the NBA. When you heard a Celtics game announced by the great Johnny Most, it was going to be from a Celtics perspective. He was an unapologetic homer, an old-school play-by-play man who called Boston games from 1953 to 1990, calling games for 16 championship teams in a style that was adored in Boston and not-so-adored in other cities. Most would openly criticize players from other teams, lambasting the Bad Boy Pistons because of their physical play against the Celtics or admonishing Magic Johnson for his complaining to officials about calls. Most is most famously known for his call on John Havlicek's steal of a Philadelphia inbounds pass during the 1965 Eastern Division Finals. He screamed, "Havlicek steals it. Over to Sam Jones. Havlicek stole the ball! It's all over! It's all over! Havlicek is being mobbed by the fans!" a phrase that Havlicek would be linked to for the rest of his life. Most was a Boston icon, the voice for a fan base that adored its team and despised opponents. There would be little criticism of the Celtics. Most would take losses hard but celebrate wins harder. He became a staple of the franchise until he stepped down at the end of the Big Three era in the late 1980s. Most was the standard for sports play-by-play announcers in an era when Americans depended heavily on radio broadcasts to bring the game home.

Johnny Most (right) poses with all-time great Lakers announcer Chick Hearn (left) and veteran announcer Fred Manfra.
COURTESY OF GETTY IMAGES

K.C. Jones Steps Down; the Franchise Decline Begins

K.C. JONES TOOK over as head coach in 1983 and led the Celtics to two NBA Championships and two other NBA Finals appearances. But the Big Three were beginning to age and deal with injuries, the Detroit Pistons with Isiah Thomas and the Chicago Bulls with Michael Jordan were emerging as contenders, and Jones felt his impact on the franchise was lessening. After being eliminated by the Pistons in the Eastern Conference Finals, Jones offered his surprising resignation as coach, accepting a position as director of player personnel. Jones would be succeeded by assistant coach Jimmy Rodgers as the franchise began a frustrating and sometimes fruitless search for a championship-caliber coach. Rodgers was fired after two seasons and then replaced by Chris Ford, who lasted five seasons. The Celtics would go through six coaches before hiring Doc Rivers, who led the club to its first title since Jones's club in 1986. Jones had a sparkling .751 winning percentage in his five seasons as Celtics coach. He would return to head coaching with the Seattle SuperSonics in 1990 and then would return to the Celtics as an assistant coach under M.L. Carr in 1996. Jones would finish his career coaching the New England Blizzard of the women's American Basketball League.

Head coach K.C. Jones looks on during a game circa 1987 at the Boston Garden.
COURTESY OF GETTY IMAGES

Larry Bird, Saves Ball, Mashes Face; Celtics Eliminate Pacers

THE EARLY 1990S Celtics were an aging bunch looking for one last spirited playoff run. Larry Bird was beginning to experience back issues and wasn't the same player as in his glory years. But he still played big in big games. In the second period of Game 5 of a first-round series against the Indiana Pacers, Bird had the ball knocked away by Indiana's Mike Sanders. The 34-year-old Bird then spun and dove for the loose ball with no consideration for his balance. He landed face-first on the floor trying to save the ball. After laying on the Garden parquet for several moments, Bird was taken to the locker room for examination. The Celtics clung onto the lead and Bird, donning his warmup jacket, sprinted up the stairs of the locker room and through the tunnel during third-quarter play, sending the crowd into a frenzy. Bird tested negative for a facial fracture and was cleared to return. Near the end of the period, an off-balance Reggie Miller collided with Bird in the precise facial area as the previous hit. In the fourth quarter, Bird took a shot to the back on a screen from Chuck Person, sending him to the floor yet again. He rose and remained in the game. Bird then helped stave off a late Indiana rally, and the Celtics prevailed with a 124–121 win. Bird scored 32 points in just 33 minutes in one of his last great playoff moments.

Indiana Pacers' Detlef Schrempf controls the ball in front of Larry Bird during Game 1 of the first round of the NBA playoffs between the Celtics and the Pacers at the Boston Garden on April 26, 1991.
COURTESY OF GETTY IMAGES

December 13, 1991: Celtics Retire No. 3 for Dennis Johnson

Dennis Johnson has his jersey retired before a game played in 1991 at the Boston Garden.
COURTESY OF GETTY IMAGES

IT ISN'T COMMON for a player to spend just seven seasons with a team and get his number retired, but Dennis Johnson was no average player. Johnson was the glue that helped the Celtics win championships in 1984 and 1986, the floor leader who sacrificed his offensive game to become a distributor, and he still had enough guile and athleticism to defend some of the league's best guards, such as Magic Johnson. Dennis Johnson was the player who immediately cut to the basket when Larry Bird stole Isiah Thomas's pass in Game 5 of the 1987 Eastern Conference Finals and made the difficult backhanded layup that won the game. Johnson was the one who could be depended on for the key jumper or key defensive stop. The Celtics acquired Johnson from the Phoenix Suns in a lopsided trade for backup center Rick Robey. He was the point guard a young, emerging Celtics team needed, and he became a wildly popular player because of that leadership and savvy. He swished the game-winning jumper that helped the Celtics win Game 4 of the 1985 NBA Finals at Los Angeles. He was the heart and soul of the Celtics. At the ceremony, Magic Johnson, just weeks after his HIV announcement, sent a congratulatory note to Dennis Johnson, while owner Red Auerbach said, "He didn't care about stats. All he wanted to do was win. He showed everything there is about being a Celtic." Johnson said Auerbach was "smart enough to make that trade for me." All of his Celtics teammates, including Bird, McHale, and Parish, came out on the floor to watch the induction.

The Last Run for the Big Three

THE END OCCURRED on May 17, 1992, at old Richfield Coliseum, in Game 7 of the Eastern Conference semifinal series against the Cleveland Cavaliers. The Celtics pushed the Cavaliers to a winner-take-all contest, but they hardly had enough to win the decisive game. The Celtics were an aging club, with Larry Bird, Kevin McHale, and Robert Parish all well over 30, and they had been passed in the Eastern Conference by the Detroit Pistons and Chicago Bulls. The Celtics lost that Game 7 122–104, ending the Big Three Era. Bird would retire after the 1991–92 season. McHale would become a reserve while Parish would play two more seasons with the Celtics before signing with the Charlotte Hornets. The trio won three championships for the Celtics and helped resurrect the reputation of the franchise after a tough stretch in the late 1970s. Bird missed three games in the Cleveland series with injuries while McHale had troublesome foot issues that hampered his production. But in their primes the Big Three combined to be one of the best trios in NBA history, and all three would reach the Naismith Memorial Basketball Hall of Fame and have their numbers raised to the rafters at Boston/TD Garden.

Mark Price #25 of the Cleveland Cavaliers shoots a jump shot over Larry Bird #33 in Game One of the Eastern Conference Semifinals during the 1992 NBA Playoffs.
COURTESY OF GETTY IMAGES

Bird Agrees to Join Dream Team for One Final Run

BACK ISSUES LIMITED Larry Bird's final season with the Celtics to 45 games. There were rumors that he would play only in home games during the 1992–93 season, but instead he decided to retire after the 1991–92 season, finishing as one of the all-time great NBA players and arguably the greatest Celtic of all time. On his way to life away from the spotlight, Bird received an intriguing offer. NBA players were finally allowed to play in international competition, and Team USA was gathering a group of players for the 1992 Olympic Games in Barcelona. NBA commissioner David Stern offered Bird a spot on that team, a swan song of sorts along with former rival Magic Johnson, who had recently retired because of his HIV diagnosis. With a chance to play with Johnson, Michael Jordan, Charles Barkley, John Stockton, Karl Malone, and several other NBA stars, Bird accepted the invitation and made his final organized basketball appearance for Team USA. Bird gathered up enough energy to play in all eight games for the Dream Team, averaging 8.3 points and shooting 52.1 percent as the Americans dominated their way to a Gold medal. It was Bird's first international appearance since 1977, when he played in the World University Games as a 20-year-old, and the opportunity to play with his peers on one of the greatest international teams ever capped off his wonderful career.

Larry Bird of Team USA answers questions from the media after practice for the men's basketball competition at the 1992 Summer Olympics in Barcelona, Spain.

COURTESY OF GETTY IMAGES

February 4, 1993, Celtics Retire Larry Bird's No. 33

IN WHAT WAS a magical night, the Celtics retired Larry Bird's No. 33 to cap off a magnificent career that resulted in three MVP awards, three NBA championships, and the resurrection of a franchise back to elite status. The Celtics decided not to hold the ceremony during halftime or on a game night, instead devoting a separate night to Bird, who showed up in his Boston Celtics warmups along with many of his former teammates, who donned their jerseys in his honor. One special guest at the ceremony was Bird's chief rival and eventual friend. Magic Johnson, who battled Bird in an NCAA championship and in three NBA Finals, made an appearance wearing his Lakers warmup suit but also a Celtics' t-shirt. The 90-minute event was more than a retirement ceremony, it was a reflection on an amazing career, with Bird talking to host Bob Costas about his most impactful moments in his Celtics career. The entire 1981 champion Celtics, including former coach Bill Fitch, greeted Bird, all wearing their warmups, with Cedric Maxwell presenting Bird with a commemorative coin. The 1984 and 1986 championship teams also greeted Bird and presented him with other mementos. Johnson and Bird then spent time reflecting on their careers and rivalry before Red Auerbach capped the evening by giving Bird his blessings. Finally, Bird's number was raised into the rafters, with Bird holding his young son as he pulled the rope and No. 33 was etched in Celtics immortality.

Larry Bird with teamates Kevin McHale and Robert Parish during Larry Bird Night at the Boston Garden on February 4, 1993.
COURTESY OF GETTY IMAGES

The Death of Reggie Lewis

SEVEN YEARS AFTER the Celtics suffered through the tragic death of Len Bias, they were handed another shocking and painful setback with the sudden death of forward Reggie Lewis. Taken in the first round of the 1987 NBA Draft out of nearby Northeastern University, Lewis was on his way to succeeding Larry Bird, Kevin McHale, and Robert Parish as a perennial All-Star when he passed away of a heart attack during a July 27, 1993 workout at Brandeis University. Lewis, who was an All-Star in 1991–92, helped the Celtics to the 1993 playoffs before collapsing during the team's opening playoff game on April 29, 1993. Lewis was initially diagnosed with a career-ending heart issue and the Celtics suggested that Lewis retire. But he received a second opinion by a doctor who believed the condition was a treatable virus and gave Lewis hope that he could play again, contradicting the medical opinion of the Celtics-assembled medical experts. While he was waiting for further treatment, Lewis decided to work out on his own at Brandeis, where he collapsed. Lewis's death devastated the Celtics' organization, which lost a beloved player and emerging star who had become popular for his community work. With the loss of Lewis, the retirements of Bird and McHale, and departure of Parish, the Celtics franchise went into a major decline from which it would take more than a decade to recover. The Celtics would retire Lewis's No. 35 on March 22, 1995, and the Reggie Lewis Center was erected in the Dorchester area of Boston as an athletic and service center for the Boston community.

Celtics senior executive vice president Dave Gavitt (top left) consoling Dee Brown (left) and Rick Fox during press interview after the death of Reggie Lewis.
COURTESY OF GETTY IMAGES

Dominique Wilkins Leads Celtics to Stunning Playoff Win Over the Mighty Magic

THERE WAS A brief time when Dominique Wilkins was a Boston Celtic. He spent the 1994–95 season in Boston after signing a one-year deal as a free agent. The mid-1990s Celtics were a team in transition, and Wilkins was acquired for veteran presence. Despite the Celtics winning just 35 games that season and finishing 12 games under .500, they reached the NBA Playoffs, facing the number one seed Orlando Magic and superstar center Shaquille O'Neal in the first round. The Celtics didn't stand much of a chance in the series, but they were able to take a game off the Magic, thanks to a throwback performance from Wilkins. Besides a Magic blowout in Game 1, the series was surprisingly competitive. In Game 2 at Orlando Arena, Wilkins scored 24 points on 10-for-17 shooting and Dee Brown added 21 as the Celtics evened the series with a 99–92 win. Wilkins would lead the Celtics in scoring for that series with 19 points along with 10.8 rebounds, showing he still had game at age 34. The Celtics would lose the series three games to one, and Wilkins would sign a contract to play the next season in Greece. The Celtics would not win another playoff game until 2002.

Dominique Wilkins looks on during a game played in 1995 at the Boston Garden.
COURTESY OF GETTY IMAGES

The interior view of the Boston Graden during a game played in 1989.
COURTESY OF GETTY IMAGES

May 5, 1995: The Last Game at the Boston Garden

THE BOSTON GARDEN was one of the toughest places to play in the NBA. Coach and team president Red Auerbach made sure the visiting locker room was either frigid or sweltering, and the shower water wasn't guaranteed to be hot. And then there was the lack of air conditioning, which took the life out of many of Celtics opponents during May and June playoff games. It was a remarkable venue, with its parquet floor and Lucky the Celtics logo at center court. But as the 1980s turned into the 1990s, it was time for a new, modern arena to house the Boston Celtics. The Celtics' final game before they moved to the nearby FleetCenter was Game 4 of the Eastern Conference first-round series against the Orlando Magic on May 5, 1995. The game was close, but the Magic won a 95-92 decision that eliminated Boston from the playoffs, and the club would move into the new arena for the 1995–96 season. Boston Garden opened in 1928, played host to the Celtics when they joined the Basketball Association of America in 1946, and was considered one of the great arenas in American sports history. Sixteen Celtics banners hung from the rafters, in addition to five banners from the NHL Boston Bruins. Auerbach would give free agents and rookies a tour of the Boston Garden and show them the history of the franchise. Boston Garden dripped with rich tradition, hosting some of the greatest events in sports history.

Celtics Put Faith in M.L. Carr

AFTER THE TRAGIC death of Reggie Lewis and the departures of Larry Bird, Kevin McHale, and Robert Parish, the Celtics were a franchise in transition. M.L. Carr, a popular former player who helped the Celtics to two championships in the 1980s, was named General Manager in 1994. Former teammate Chris Ford, who had been named coach in 1990, couldn't lead the Celtics to their past glory. Carr decided to fire Ford, despite having signed him to a contract extension the prior year, and name himself as the head coach for the 1995–96 season. By this time the Celtics were undergoing a youth movement, and they were unable to achieve any real chemistry or consistency on the floor. For decades the Celtics had been able to find a championship core with the great years far outnumbering the lean years, but these were lean years. The Celtics were losing their way. During the 1996–97 season, the Celtics decided that it was best to plan for the 1997 draft, featuring Wake Forest University center Tim Duncan. That Celtics team won a franchise-worst 15 games but did not win the NBA draft lottery, losing out to the San Antonio Spurs. President Red Auerbach decided to make major changes after that season, firing Carr and hiring University of Kentucky coach Rick Pitino.

The Celtics try out Kobe Bryant. Here he chats with M.L. Carr during the workout.
COURTESY OF GETTY IMAGES

Rick Fox #44 posts up during a game played on February 2, 1997 at Continental Airlines Arena in East Rutherford, NJ.
COURTESY OF GETTY IMAGES

Rick Fox Shows Potential. Finishes Fifth in Steals

THE 1996–97 SEASON was a tough one in Boston. The Celtics were in total rebuild mode, hoping to land the number 1 pick in the 1997 draft, projected to be Wake Forest University center Tim Duncan. But while the Celtics were going through this painful process, swingman Rick Fox emerged as a defensive standout. In what would be his final year in Boston, Fox set a club record with 167 steals on a 15-win team. Fox had six steals in a game on three different occasions and finished fifth in the NBA in that category that season.

His 2.2 steals per game would be by far the highest total of his 13-year career, and he broke Larry Bird's previous record of 166 steals. Teammate David Wesley added 162 steals for Boston in 1996–97. Fox's record would last until 2010, when Rajon Rondo collected 189 steals, a mark that still stands. There were few bright spots during that difficult era in Celtics basketball, but Fox's defensive prowess was one of them.

The Rick Pitino Era

DESPERATE FOR A big-name coach after years of losing, the Celtics made a bold move in replacing M.L. Carr as head coach. Rick Pitino had just led the University of Kentucky to a national championship in 1996 and another Final Four in '97. He was the hottest NBA coaching prospect on the market, and the Celtics decided to offer Pitino a 10-year, $70 million contract to be their coach and president of basketball operations. The Celtics hired Pitino on May 6, 1997, and gave him authority to make personnel decisions as well as coach the team. The marriage seemed as if it was the right idea. But Pitino never quite adapted to the NBA game, and he grew impatient with the Celtics' rebuilding plan, the pressure to revive the franchise, and expectations from fans because of his salary. The Celtics expected results from their investment in Pitino, and he was unable to produce a winning record or a playoff appearance in his three-plus seasons. While the Pitino era in Boston did not reap the expected results, there were a myriad of issues in the organization, including injuries, the Celtics' inability to draw free agents, and the failure of players such as Ron Mercer and Kenny Anderson to emerge as cornerstones. Pitino was able to help develop the duo of Paul Pierce and Antoine Walker, and those two would later take the Celtics to an Eastern Conference Finals in 2002. But the Pitino era is viewed as unsuccessful for both sides because he was frustrated by the NBA dynamics, his college style never translated to the highest level, and—because he was given full control of roster decisions—he shouldered the blame for the team's struggles. The Celtics had not won a championship in more than a decade, and the all-time great players on those 1980s rosters were long gone. Pitino's lack of success was a lesson that not all great college coaches are meant to coach in the NBA. He finished with a 102–146 record in his stretch before resigning after 34 games in 2001.

Guard Chris Herren and coach Rick Pitino's expressions on the bench reflect their loss against the 76ers.
COURTESY OF GETTY IMAGES

Giving Up On Chauncey Billups

THE CELTICS PREPARED during the 1996–97 season to score big in the 1997 draft. They decided to go through a total rebuild, sacrificing wins for talent development to give themselves the best chance to select Wake Forest center Tim Duncan, unquestionably the best prospect in the draft. Instead, the Celtics, despite the league's worst record, did not win the draft lottery, falling to the third pick. With that selection, the Celtics opted for Colorado sophomore Chauncey Billups, a physically skilled but raw prospect. New coach Rick Pitino, who had also taken over for M.L. Carr as coach and president of basketball operations, had little patience for the young Billups. Billups played just 51 games for the Celtics and in an extremely rare move, Pitino decided to trade his just-drafted lottery pick to the Toronto Raptors along with the popular Dee Brown in a deal that netted former lottery pick Kenny Anderson. Pitino wanted a savvier point guard and felt the young Billups was disposable. Billups went on to have a 17-year career, reach five All-Star Games, winning a championship with the Detroit Pistons and earning the moniker, 'Mr. Big Shot.' In 2024, he was elected into the Naismith Memorial Basketball Hall of Fame. Pitino would say years later he regretted giving up on Billups so quickly as the trade to get Anderson did not result in much success for the Celtics. Billups would bounce around the NBA, playing for Toronto, Minnesota, and Denver before finding a home in Detroit.

Chauncey Billups dribbles during the Rookie All-Star Game played February 7, 1998 at Madison Square Garden.
COURTESY OF GETTY IMAGES

Larry Bird Returns to Boston as Coach of the Pacers

LARRY BIRD DECIDED he wanted to pursue coaching after his retirement and accepted the Pacers job in his native Indiana in May 1997. The Celtics all-time great made his return to Boston on January 18, 1998, under drastically different circumstances than when he played. The Celtics had vacated Boston Garden and now played in new nearby FleetCenter. Only one player on the Celtics roster—Dee Brown—had played with Bird before his retirement in 1992. In his typical fashion, Bird completely tried to downplay the moment. He walked out onto the floor to the theme of "Welcome Back Kotter" and the crowd reacted with a standing ovation. Bird reluctantly accepted the ovation and raised his hand in acknowledgement. But he wanted to focus on the game and the other event that night, the jersey retirement of former teammate Robert Parish at halftime. "If the game was played next door [at the Boston Garden], it would be different," Bird said when asked before the game whether the moment would be emotional. "I have absolutely no ties to this building." According to the *Baltimore Sun*, Bird added: "To me, we're playing a different Celtic team. There's really no one, other than Dee Brown, that I really know. For me, emotionally, playing against the Boston Celtics really doesn't mean a lot. Playing for the Celtics meant a lot." The Pacers held on for a 103–96 win against a rebuilding Celtics team, and Bird then expressed his true emotions afterward. "It was just so awesome to be out there today," he said. "I remember the first time I came here and told [the fans] I would play through pain and do my best to win championships for them. I feel like I held up to my promise. And they held up to theirs."

Larry Bird, head coach of the Indiana Pacers and former Celtics star, waves to his old fans in Boston before Indiana's game against the Celtics at the FleetCenter.

COURTESY OF GETTY IMAGES

The Celtics Luck Into Drafting Paul Pierce

PAUL PIERCE WAS an All-American at the University of Kansas during his junior season and was projected to be a top 5 pick in the 1998 NBA Draft. The Celtics, drafting 10th after going 36–46, held little hope of landing Pierce with their pick. But something funny happened on draft night. For unknown reasons, Pierce's stock began to fall. Perhaps it was because he wasn't an elite athlete. The slippage began when Dallas selected Michigan's Robert Traylor sixth and then Sacramento, located in Pierce's home state, opted for Florida point guard Jason Williams. Philadelphia passed on Pierce by taking Saint Louis University guard Larry Hughes. Milwaukee eventually took a little known German prospect named Dirk Nowitzki ninth (they would eventually trade him to Dallas for the rights to Traylor). With the 10th pick, Pierce was sitting there and available. Celtics coach Rick Pitino had his heart set on taking Nowitzki, convinced Boston was the only club that knew about his talent until the Mavericks pulled off a draft-day deal with Milwaukee to get the German sensation. The Celtics coach quickly bounced back by taking Pierce, who hadn't even conducted a pre-draft workout for Boston because Pitino assumed he wouldn't last until 10. Celtics General Manager Chris Wallace told the *Boston Globe*, "I never dreamed we'd get Paul Pierce. I felt Paul was one of the top three players in the draft, and it just shows you it's better to be lucky than good." Pierce would play 15 seasons with the Celtics and reach the Naismith Memorial Basketball Hall of Fame.

Paul Pierce poses for a photo after being selected by the Celtics at the 1998 NBA Draft in New York.
COURTESY OF GETTY IMAGES

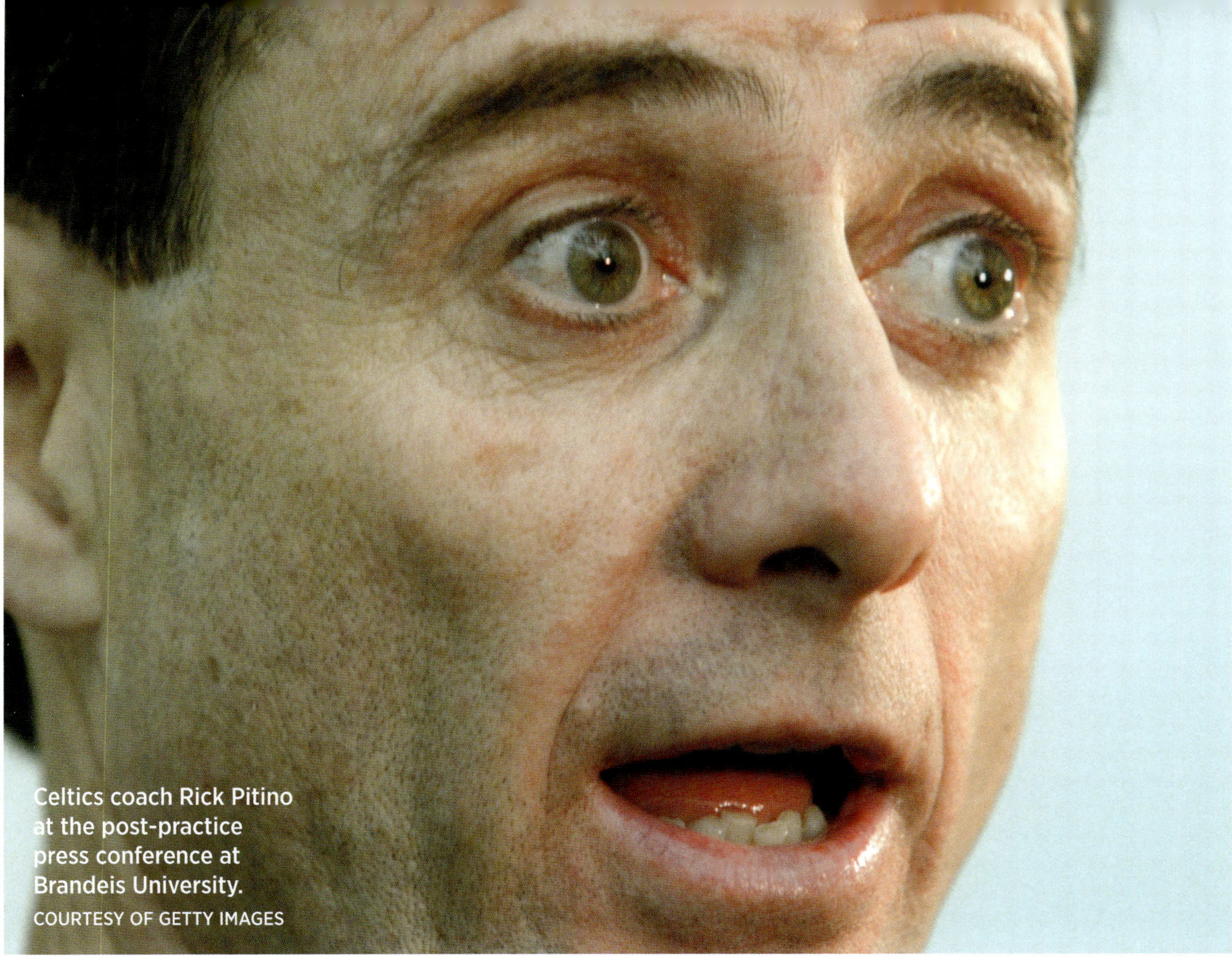

Celtics coach Rick Pitino at the post-practice press conference at Brandeis University.
COURTESY OF GETTY IMAGES

"They Are Not Walking Through That Door"

AFTER A TOUGH, last-second loss to the Toronto Raptors on March 1, 2000, Celtics coach Rick Pitino addressed the media and appeared completely dejected about the state of the franchise. There had been expectations when he took over in May 1997. The former University of Kentucky coach had built a powerhouse program and won an NCAA championship. He appeared to have the savvy and basketball acumen to resuscitate the Celtics' franchise, but it just wasn't working. In an act of frustration, Pitino strongly urged Celtics fans to stop living in the past and expecting championships in an NBA that was so dramatically different than the glory days. He told reporters: "Larry Bird is not walking through that door, fans. Kevin McHale is not walking through that door, and Robert Parish is not walking through that door. And if you expect them to walk through that door, they're going to be gray and old. What we are is young, exciting, hard-working, and we're going to improve. People don't realize that, and as soon as they realize those three guys are not coming through that door, the better this town will be for all of us because there are young guys in that (locker) room playing their asses off. I wish we had $90 million under the salary cap. I wish we could buy the world. We can't; the only thing we can do is work hard, and all the negativity that's in this town sucks. I've been around when Jim Rice was booed. I've been around when (Carl) Yastrzemski was booed. And it stinks. It makes the greatest town, greatest city in the world, lousy. The only thing that will turn this around is being upbeat and positive like we are in that locker room . . . and if you think I'm going to succumb to negativity, you're wrong. You've got the wrong guy leading this basketball team." Pitino would resign 34 games into the 2000–01 season.

The Milt Palacio Game, December 28, 2000

IT WAS HIS only shot and only make of the game, but it occurred at the perfect time to save the Celtics on a chilly night in East Rutherford, New Jersey. The Celtics looked done against the New Jersey Nets, trailing by two points with 1.8 seconds left and Nets' ball at midcourt. The Celtics were scrambling on defense, hoping for a New Jersey miscue, and it happened. Inbounder Lucious Harris threw behind a streaking Aaron Williams, allowing Milt Palacio, a undrafted free-agent guard from Colorado State, to catch the ball and the fire a 30-footer in the same motion. The ball rattled through the hoop and it was mayhem for the Celtics, who all converged on the stunned Palacio and celebrated their improbable 112–111 victory. Palacio had played 17 previous minutes in that game but had not attempted a shot. And it was the shining moment for the journeyman who played 470 games with six NBA teams. Palacio played 99 games with the Celtics and averaged 5 points per game, but he may not have hit a bigger shot in his career.

Milt Palacio waits for the tip off during a preseason game against the Charlotte Hornets.

COURTESY OF GETTY IMAGES

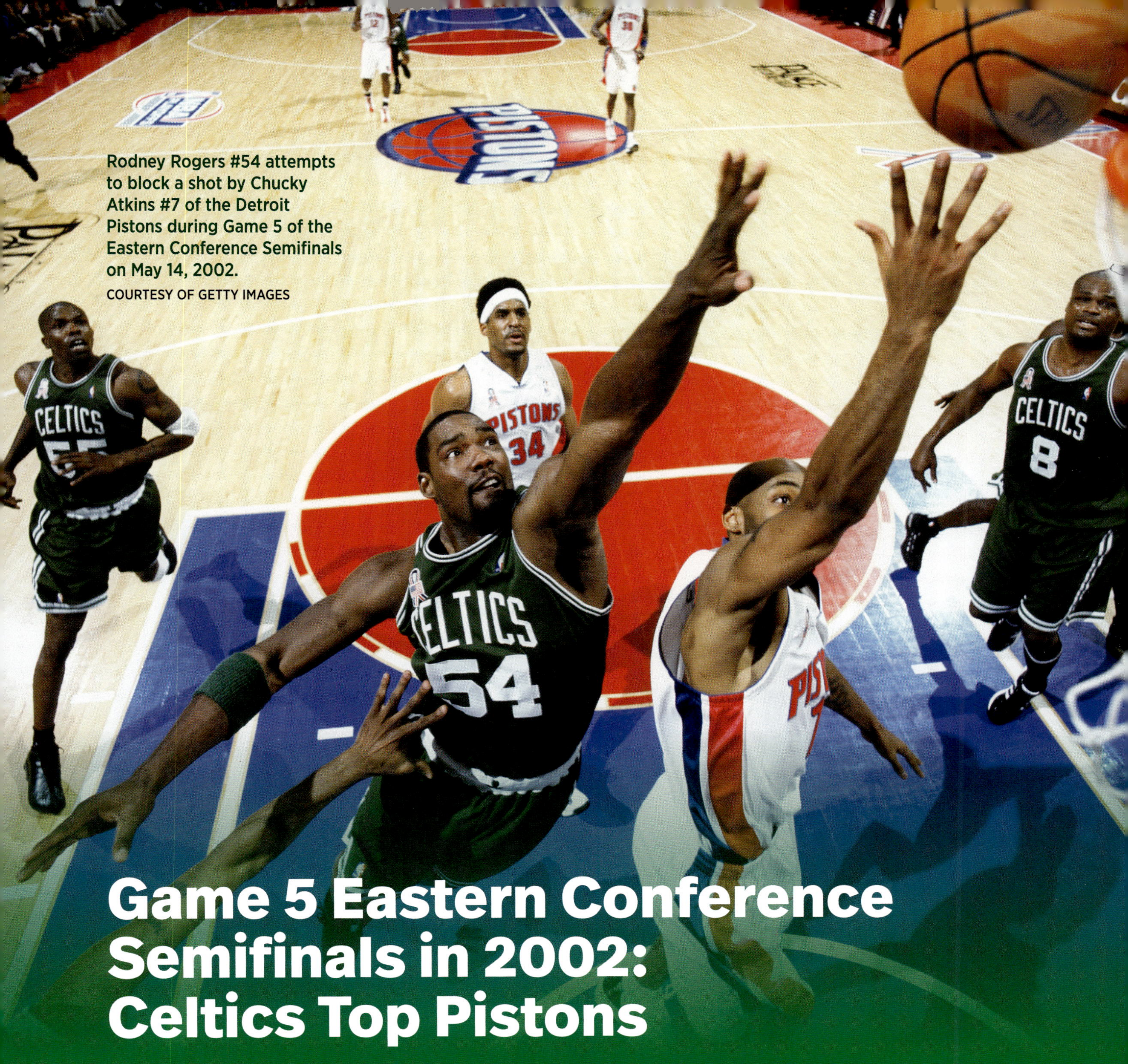

Rodney Rogers #54 attempts to block a shot by Chucky Atkins #7 of the Detroit Pistons during Game 5 of the Eastern Conference Semifinals on May 14, 2002.
COURTESY OF GETTY IMAGES

Game 5 Eastern Conference Semifinals in 2002: Celtics Top Pistons

THE CELTICS WERE experiencing a renaissance in 2002 under coach Jim O'Brien. A year after Rick Pitino abruptly resigned, the Celtics began galvanizing as a franchise led by Paul Pierce, Antoine Walker, and Kenny Anderson. The result was their first playoff appearance in seven years and their first series win in 10 years. The Celtics unseated the defending Eastern Conference champion Philadelphia 76ers in the first round before facing the upstart Detroit Pistons in the semifinals. The series wasn't close. The Celtics defeated the Pistons in five games, including an impressive closeout win on the road at the Palace of Auburn Hills. The Boston defense held the Pistons to 35 percent shooting. The Celtics won this series with defense. After losing Game 1, the Celtics did not yield more than 81 points in any of the final four games. Boston managed to beat the Pistons 66–64 in the lowest-scoring game in modern playoff history. Both teams combined to shoot 4-for-39 from the 3-point line, and they combined for 38 turnovers. Still, the Celtics won consecutive playoff series for the first time since 1988 and earned a matchup with the New Jersey Nets in the Eastern Conference Finals.

Pierce Leads the Celtics from 26 Down to Beat Nets in Eastern Conference Finals

THE CELTICS FINALLY climbed back into being playoff contention in the early 2000s behind the duo of Paul Pierce and Antoine Walker. Boston entered the 2002 playoffs as the third seed after winning 49 games, and it beat the defending Eastern Conference champion Philadelphia 76ers in the first round and then topped the Detroit Pistons in the second round for the right to meet the top-seeded New Jersey Nets. The Celtics split the first two games of that series, beating the Nets in New Jersey in Game 2. Back in Boston for Game 3, the Nets raced out to a 65–39 lead with 8:30 left in the third quarter, and the Celtics looked done. But Pierce wasn't going to allow the Celtics to give up. He fueled a stunning comeback in the final quarter, scoring 19 of his 28 points as Boston outscored the overwhelmed Nets 41–16 for a 94–90 win, one of the greatest comebacks in franchise history. After the victory, Pierce broke free of his teammates and jumped on to the scorer's table to celebrate with the fans. The Celtics had been suffering most of the past decade, and Pierce played a significant role in the organization's resurrection in their biggest playoff win since the Larry Bird days. It was the moment that Pierce became the face of the franchise and the Celtics were no longer laughingstocks. With a chance to take control of the series, the Celtics lost Game 4 at home as the Nets went on to win the series. But a return to the Eastern Conference Finals after a 14-year absence was a welcomed accomplishment for Celtics faithful.

Paul Pierce #34 and Antoine Walker during the Eastern Conference Finals versus the New Jersey Nets, East Rutherford, New Jersey in May, 2002.
COURTESY OF GETTY IMAGES

Pierce Outduels Al Harrington in 2003

PAUL PIERCE HAS never been a humble player. He became a franchise cornerstone with his confident style. After the Celtics reached the Eastern Conference Finals in 2002, they returned to the postseason in 2003, facing the Indiana Pacers in the first round. In the third quarter of Game 4, with the Celtics leading 70–62, Pierce dribbled down the clock for the final shot of the third period, with Indiana's Al Harrington facing up defensively. Pierce and Harrington began trash talking, seemingly the only ones on the schoolyard, but the NBA world was watching. Pierce, talking for the entire time, decided to dribble with his right hand, dart left and then launch a 3-pointer in the final 10 seconds of the period. The result: swish. The exchange was legendary and it added to the reputation of Pierce, who became known for his clutch scoring and big-time shot making. The Celtics would go on to win the game and the series, with Pierce leading the Celtics in scoring at 25.8 points per game and 40 percent from the 3-point line. It was another signature Pierce moment.

Paul Pierce #34 shoots over Al Harrington of the Indiana Pacers in the first round of the Eastern Conference playoffs at FleetCenter on April 27, 2003.
COURTESY OF GETTY IMAGES

Danny Ainge Returns to Run the Show

RED AUERBACH WANTED to put the Celtics' organization in good hands. He wanted stability after the Celtics' attempt to make Rick Pitino coach and president of basketball operations had failed. Auerbach looked back to the organization's glorious past for his next franchise leader. Danny Ainge had spent parts of four seasons coaching the Phoenix Suns before jumping into television commentating with Turner Sports. Ainge could have taken other jobs with better prospects, but on May 9, 2003, he officially accepted the position as president of basketball operations, running the team where he won two NBA championships and was a fan favorite as a player. Majority owner Wyc Grousbeck made the move during the Celtics–Nets Eastern Conference semifinals because he did not want to lose Ainge to the Portland Trail Blazers, who were also in search of a general manager. The situation was difficult. The Celtics were a team trying to return to prominence behind Paul Pierce and Antoine Walker, but they needed a solid coach. One of Ainge's first moves was to hire Doc Rivers as head coach. Ainge then rebuilt the roster around Pierce and then made two of the biggest acquisitions in franchise history by bringing in Kevin Garnett and Ray Allen in the summer of 2007. Ainge spent 18 years as Celtics president of basketball operations, bringing the Celtics a championship in 2008 and another NBA Finals appearance in 2010. Ainge earned the moniker "Trader Danny" for his desire to reshape the Celtics roster with major trades.

Hall of Fame coach Red Auerbach and executive director of operations for the Celtics Danny Ainge make their way onto the court prior to Game 3 of the Eastern Conference Semifinals versus the New Jersey Nets in 2003.
COURTESY OF GETTY IMAGES

Red Auerbach, vice chairman of the board for the Celtics, smokes one of his trademark cigars in a 1996 portrait in Boston.
COURTESY OF GETTY IMAGES

Passing of Red Auerbach

RED AUERBACH'S IMPACT on the Celtics franchise is immeasurable. From a Hall of Fame coach to a top-notch general manager and president, Auerbach was synonymous with not only Celtics basketball but also the growth and expansion of the NBA. After his coaching stint from 1950 to 1966, Auerbach became the team's general manager until 1984, when he was promoted to president and stepped back from day-to-day operations. Auerbach was the godfather of the Celtics franchise acquiring or drafting Bill Russell, John Havlicek, Dave Cowens, Jo Jo White, and Larry Bird. He made shrewd trades such as acquiring Robert Parish and the draft pick that became Kevin McHale from the Warriors, getting Dennis Johnson from the Phoenix Suns, and getting Quinn Buckner from the Bucks for the rights to the retired Cowens. He also drafted the NBA's first Black player and named Russell as the league's first Black coach. Auerbach took a step back from the organization in his later years, becoming a sort of president emeritus and helping out with some of the decision making, such as convincing former player Danny Ainge to return to the organization as a general manager. Auerbach passed away on October 28, 2006, just three days after receiving an award for his service in the Naval Academy. The Celtics retired No. 2 in honor of Auerbach on January 4, 1985, shortly after he retired as general manager. Auerbach was inducted into the Naismith Memorial Basketball Hall of Fame in 1969 as a coach. The city of Boston named the North Station concourse after Auerbach in 2010, and the Celtics named their new practice facility in suburban Boston "The Auerbach Center" in honor of the most impactful person in the history of the franchise.

Celtics Hire Doc Rivers

DOC RIVERS HAD every intention of going back to television and taking some time off when he was fired by the Orlando Magic after a 1–10 start in November 2003. He had led the Magic to three consecutive playoff appearances but never advanced past the first round. Danny Ainge, a former rival of Rivers during their playing days, was looking for a head coach after the team dismissed Jim O'Brien during the 2003–04 season. Ainge thought Rivers would be a perfect fit to help resurrect the franchise. Rivers was still only 43 years old and was considered a rising young coach before injury issues to Grant Hill and Tracy McGrady's unhappiness halted his momentum with the Magic. Rivers agreed to coach the Celtics on April 28, 2004, just days after Ainge said he would take his time to search for a new coach. Ainge admitted he had Rivers in mind when the position opened, and it would be the beginning of a beautiful marriage as, after two difficult seasons, Rivers would lead the Celtics to their 17th NBA championship in 2008 and another NBA Finals appearance in 2010. Rivers coached the Celtics for nine seasons, helping bring the franchise back to respectability. The Celtics reached the playoffs in seven of Rivers's nine seasons. He was named head coach of the Eastern Conference team in the All-Star Game twice while with the Celtics and was also named among the top 15 NBA coaches of all time.

Head coach Doc Rivers and president of basketball operations Danny Ainge celebrate after defeating the Los Angeles Lakers in Game 6 of the NBA Finals on June 17, 2008 at TD Banknorth Garden.
COURTESY OF GETTY IMAGES

Ray Allen #20 celebrates after scoring against the Orlando Magic (with Kendrick Perkins close behind) on March 8, 2009 at TD Banknorth Garden.
COURTESY OF GETTY IMAGES

Kendrick Perkins

KENDRICK PERKINS HAD potential, but it wasn't going to be realized right away. Perkins was a mammoth prep standout from Texas who decided to enter the draft as an 18-year-old. The rebuilding Celtics decided to acquire Perkins on draft night 2003, knowing it would take a few years for the big man to develop. After two full seasons where he saw limited action, Perkins became a starter in the middle for the 2005–06 season and would become a staple for the Celtics for the next six years. Perkins was an enforcer, a big body who could protect the paint, rebound, and even hit the short jumper. When the Celtics acquired Kevin Garnett in 2007, they were able to slide the perennial All-Star into his desired power forward position, teaming him with Perkins for the best defensive frontcourt in the NBA. Perkins was a key contributor in the Celtics' 2008 championship, but his impact may have been felt more in 2010, when Boston needed one win in its final two games in Los Angeles to earn a second title in three years. Perkins tore his ACL in Game 6 against the Lakers, and the Celtics defense suffered. Boston lost the series in seven games, and Celtics faithful wondered if they would have won the series with a healthy Perkins. He didn't fill up the stat sheet or wow fans with his athleticism, but Perkins was a stellar defender and wouldn't mind giving a hard foul or two to make a statement.

Celtics Acquire Rajon Rondo on Draft Night

AS THE 2006 NBA draft approached, the Celtics were eyeing a franchise-changing point guard, and president of basketball operations Danny Ainge targeted a gangly but skilled standout from the University of Kentucky named Rajon Rondo. Ainge had already used the seventh overall pick in 2006 to trade for former high school sensation Sebastian Telfair and didn't have another first-round pick. Instead, he decided to trade the team's second first-round pick in 2007 to the Phoenix Suns for the rights to Rondo. Rondo was known as a player who would at times clash with Kentucky coach Tubby Smith but also possessed uncanny confidence and a brilliant basketball mind. The trade would eventually be recognized as one of Ainge's finest during his tenure with the Celtics.

In his second season, an unproven Rondo showed he was capable of being the floor leader for the 2007–08 championship team that included perennial All-Stars Kevin Garnett, Ray Allen, and Paul Pierce. Rondo also made four All-Star Games with Boston, led the NBA in assists three times, and finished fourth all-time in total assists in franchise history. Rondo is the Celtics' franchise leader in assists per game with 8.49 and set a career high with 24 assists on October 29, 2010. He also emerged as a fiery leader, a big-time playoff performer, and one of the primary contributors to the team's revival in the late 2000s.

Rajon Rondo poses for a portrait during Media Day on October 6, 2006, at the Celtics' practice facility in Waltham, Massachusetts.
COURTESY OF GETTY IMAGES

Paul Pierce Drops a Career High 50 Points at Cleveland, February 15, 2006

IT WAS A SHOOTOUT between two of the game's great small forwards and a prelude to a rivalry that would last nearly a decade. On a February night in Boston, LeBron James and Paul Pierce got into an entertaining duel that resulted in a thrilling game that took two overtimes to decide. James, in his third NBA season, scored 43 points along with 12 rebounds and 11 assists. Pierce exceeded those scoring totals with 50 points, 7 rebounds, and 8 assists in a whopping 54 minutes in a 113–109 loss. Pierce reached the free throw line 20 times and carried the Celtics throughout that game. The 2005–06 Celtics were in rebuilding mode, with the 28-year-old Pierce being the main attraction under coach Doc Rivers. Pierce was the first Celtic to score 50 points in a game since Larry Bird had accomplished the feat in 1989. The 2005–06 season was one of the more efficient years in Pierce's career to that point, and he said he considered asking for a trade before a conversation with owner Wyc Grousbeck, who committed to putting a winning product on the floor. A year later, the Celtics acquired Kevin Garnett and Ray Allen and began a new Big Three era.

The Celtics' Paul Pierce #34 goes hard against LeBron James #23 of the Cleveland Cavaliers February 15, 2006 at TD Banknorth Garden. The Cavs defeated the Celtics 113–109 in double overtime.
COURTESY OF GETTY IMAGES

Gerald Green Wins Dunk Contest

THE CELTICS tried building a young core around Paul Pierce, and one of those potential cornerstones was high-school product Gerald Green, a first-round pick out of Gulf Shores Academy in Houston. Green was a raw player but possessed tremendous athleticism, and in his second season he was selected for the Slam Dunk Contest at All-Star Weekend in Las Vegas. At the league's midseason showcase, Green shined with his acrobatic dunks, including catching a pass off the side of the backboard from teammate Pierce and jamming it down easily with two hands. On his second dunk, wearing a Dee Brown jersey, Green soared over fellow participant Nate Robinson for a one-handed hammer dunk, earning kudos from the star-studded judges—Michael Jordan, Dominique Wilkins, Julius Erving, Vince Carter, and Kobe Bryant. Green finished the contest by jumping over a table in the middle of the key and completing a windmill dunk. The judges all gave Green 10s for his effort, making him the second Celtic to win the Slam Dunk Contest, edging Robinson. Brown had been the first Celtic to take the honor with his famous no-look dunk in 1991.

Gerald Green dunks over a table in the finals of the Sprite Slam Dunk Competition at NBA All-Star Weekend on February 17, 2007 at Thomas & Mack Center in Las Vegas, Nevada.
COURTESY OF GETTY IMAGES

2007–08 Team Starts 29–3

USUALLY IT TAKES teams that add multiple impact players a few months to establish chemistry and cohesion. That wasn't the case for the 2007–08 Celtics, who got off to a running start in their first season with Paul Pierce, Kevin Garnett, and Ray Allen as a trio. Using a preseason trip to Rome and London to galvanize, the Celtics were dominant from the opening tip of the season, racing to a 29–3 start, a stretch that included two nine-game winning streaks and an eight-game streak. It was the fourth-best three-loss start in NBA history. The Celtics started the season by winning their first eight games before a 2-point loss against the rival Orlando Magic, and then five games later, ran off nine more in a row. The combined losing margin of their first three losses was just nine points, including an overtime loss to LeBron James and the Cleveland Cavaliers. Later in the season, the Celtics would add winning streaks of 10 and seven games en route to 66 wins and the number one seed in the Eastern Conference. And they would go on to win the franchise's first title in 22 years.

Kevin Garnett #5, Paul Pierce #34, and Ray Allen #20 (left to right) during a game against the Orlando Magic at Amway Arena on November 18, 2007 in Orlando, Florida.
COURTESY OF GETTY IMAGES

Paul Pierce Wheelchair Game, June 5, 2008

IN GAME 1 of the NBA Finals, the Celtics first appearance in the championship in 21 years, forward Paul Pierce was flourishing against his hometown team, the Los Angeles Lakers. Pierce was besting rival Kobe Bryant as the two teams went back and forth into the second half. With the Lakers leading 62–58 at the 6:49 mark of the third quarter, Pierce collided with teammate Kendrick Perkins and landed awkwardly on his right knee. Pierce fell to the floor in front of the Celtics' bench writhing in pain as the sold-out crowd at TD Garden went silent. He was then carried to the locker room tunnel by teammates Brian Scalabrine and Tony Allen, and team doctor Brian McKeon called for a wheelchair at the end of the tunnel. A television camera caught Pierce being carted to the locker room for treatment, with Celtics faithful fearing a series-ending injury. That wasn't the case. At the 5:35 mark of the third quarter, a little more than one minute of playing time later, Pierce skipped through the tunnel back onto the floor, when the crowd went into a frenzy. He checked back in at the 5:04 mark and later added a pair of 3-pointers to put the Celtics ahead. Pierce finished with 22 points on 7-for-10 shooting as the Celtics pulled away for a 98–88 win. Pierce told reporters initially he feared a torn knee ligament but once he returned into the locker room and could put weight on the leg, he was ready to return.

Paul Pierce #34 returns to the court after being taken off in a wheelchair in the third quarter of Game One of the 2008 NBA Finals against the Los Angeles Lakers.
COURTESY OF GETTY IMAGES

Paul Pierce dumps Gatorade on head coach Doc Rivers after the Celtics defeated the Los Angeles Lakers in Game 6 of the NBA Finals on June 17, 2008 at TD Banknorth Garden.
COURTESY OF GETTY IMAGES

Anything is Possible! Celtics Win it All in 2008

DANNY AINGE DIDN'T want to wait until high draft picks developed into stars. He had tried that already, and the Celtics were a franchise that needed immediate help. So he made daring moves to acquire Kevin Garnett and Ray Allen to join Paul Pierce. He also added veterans such as Sam Cassell, Eddie House, and P.J. Brown to build a championship contender, and the Celtics did not disappoint. Behind the leadership of Garnett, pinpoint shooting of Allen, and clutch play of Pierce, the Celtics immediately became championship favorites. They ran off to a 29–3 record and eventually won 66 games, entering the playoffs as the number one seed. But the postseason would not be as easy. The Celtics were pushed to seven games in the first round by the upstart Atlanta Hawks before hammering the Hawks in Game 7 at home. They were pushed to the brink by LeBron James and the Cleveland Cavaliers before edging the Cavs 97–92 in an epic Game 7 win. The Celtics then essentially ended the Eastern Conference dominance of the Detroit Pistons by ousting them in six games, sealing the series on the road for their first NBA Finals appearance in 21 years. There was a familiar foe waiting for the Celtics. The Los Angeles Lakers, behind Kobe Bryant, had rebuilt after the departure of Shaquille O'Neal and returned to the NBA Finals for the first time in four years. But the Celtics would win this edition of the rivalry. A team of destiny that was put together to bring Boston back to the top of the basketball world would not be denied. After winning the first two games, the Celtics dropped Game 3 at Staples Center and trailed 45–21 in Game 4, but behind Allen and reserves James Posey and Leon Powe, the Celtics mounted a spirited rally to tie the game at 73 and eventually won 97–91. In Game 6, the Celtics gave their home fans the elusive title after 22 seasons, blowing out the Lakers and giving Garnett, Allen, and Pierce their first titles. "Anything is possible!" Garnett screamed in a quote that has become one of the most popular in NBA history.

The Game 4 Comeback

THE 2008 CELTICS had a habit of making matters harder for themselves during the postseason, and Game 4 of the NBA Finals against the Los Angeles Lakers was no different. After taking two games in Boston, the Celtics lost a close Game 3 decision in Los Angeles. The Lakers then punched first in Game 4, jumping out to a 45–21 lead behind Lamar Odom and Pau Gasol. It was only halfway through the second quarter and coach Doc Rivers implored his team to value every possession and start a methodical rally. James Posey and Ray Allen sparked a quick 10–0 run, and the Celtics got within striking distance by halftime (58–40). The Celtics couldn't make up any ground early in the third quarter and trailed by 20 until Paul Pierce began a stunning run with a layup followed by an Eddie House 3-pointer. Posey and Allen added baskets. House added another 3-pointer. P.J. Brown brought the Celtics to within two with a dunk and Leon Powe finally tied the game at 73 with a short jumper, completing a 25–5 run. House followed with a jumper to give the Celtics their first lead with 4:07 left. Posey added a 3-pointer, and Allen sealed the comeback with a layup with 16.4 seconds left as the Celtics won 97–91. They took control of the series with a 76–46 run in the final two-and-a-half quarters, the largest comeback in the NBA Finals in 37 years.

Paul Pierce #34 and Ray Allen #20 celebrate against the Los Angeles Lakers during Game Four of the NBA Finals at the Staples Center on June 12, 2008.

COURTESY OF GETTY IMAGES

Kevin Garnett #5 defends LeBron James of the Cleveland Cavaliers in Game 7 of the Eastern Conference Semifinals during the NBA Playoffs at TD Banknorth Garden on May 18, 2008.
COURTESY OF GETTY IMAGES

KG Wins Defensive Player of the Year

KEVIN GARNETT BROUGHT instant credibility to a Boston franchise that needed a culture change. Most of that culture was built defensively, as Garnett enjoyed a brilliant first season in Boston, 2007–08. Garnett already had been a perennial All-Defensive Team selection, but he elevated his game, becoming the free safety of the Celtics defense orchestrated by associate coach Tom Thibodeau. Garnett finally received his long-awaited Defensive Player of the Year Award after 13 seasons. Garnett helped the Celtics become the number two scoring defense (90.3 points) and number one field goal percentage defense (41.9 percent) in the NBA that season. With Garnett barking commands to his teammates, the Celtics turned into a stifling defense, getting help from big man Kendrick Perkins and point guard Rajon Rondo. Garnett even demanded that Paul Pierce and Ray Allen, known more for their scoring, become more defensively engaged, and the result was one of the best defensive teams in Celtics history. Garnett's defensive rating was just 94 (points per 100 possessions), the second-lowest total of his career. There were some questions as to whether Garnett's best basketball had been played during his first 12 years in Minnesota, but he quickly squelched those concerns with a career season and his first Defensive Player of the Year Award after being selected six times to the All-Defensive First Team.

Garnett's Knee Won't Allow for a Repeat

THE CELTICS WON an NBA championship in their first season with the trio of Kevin Garnett, Ray Allen, and Paul Pierce, and they were looking for a repeat in the 2008–09 season. There was no hangover for the defending champions, as they began the season with a 27–2 record, including a franchise-record 19-game winning streak. They reached the All-Star Break with a 44–11 record after a win at Dallas. The second half of the season kicked off in Utah, and that's where everything changed. Garnett, who had stayed remarkably healthy throughout his career, left the Utah game with knee soreness that eventually was diagnosed as a bone spur. After missing 13 games to treat the injury, Garnett returned for a brief four-game stretch in March. But he continued to experience soreness and was shut down for the rest of the season. With Glen "Big Baby" Davis in the starting lineup to replace Garnett, the Celtics went on to win 62 games. They were the second seed in the playoffs, but after defeating a young Derrick Rose and the Chicago Bulls in seven games, they ran into the rising Orlando Magic and superstar center Dwight Howard. The Celtics sorely missed Garnett's defense in that series, and the Magic prevailed in the Eastern Conference semifinals, beating an exhausted Boston team 101–82 in Game 7 at TD Garden and ending its quest for a repeat. Even today, Celtics faithful wonder what might have happened if Garnett had been healthy for that season.

Paul Pierce (left) and an injured Kevin Garnett watch the action from the bench in Game 1 of the Eastern Conference Quarterfinals against the Chicago Bulls during the 2009 NBA Playoffs.
COURTESY OF GETTY IMAGES

Who's the Champ? Paul Pierce Wins the 2010 3-Point Contest

PAUL PIERCE HAS always been considered a scorer but never a real shooter. He always felt his shooting skills were undervalued, especially from the 3-point line. Pierce's 3-point percentage fluctuated throughout the years, but he was shooting at a solid 37 percent when he was invited to participate in the 2010 3-Point Contest at All-Star Weekend in Dallas, where Larry Bird won his first 3-Point Contest. Pierce scored a 17 to advance to the Final against Golden State sharpshooter Stephen Curry and Denver's Chauncey Billups. In the Final, Pierce scored 20 to edge Curry (17) and Billups (14) to earn his first 3-point title. The victory made up for Pierce's 2002 performance, where he was eliminated in the first round with just eight points. After being presented with the trophy, Pierce walked through the tunnel and American Airlines Center chanting, "Who's the champ?" For Pierce it was further evidence that he had turned himself into a premium shooter throughout his career. His 1,823 3-pointers made were a Celtics record, and he is 14th all-time in 3-pointers with 2,143. What's more, Pierce's final shot at TD Garden, as a member of the Los Angeles Clippers, was a 3-pointer.

Paul Pierce wins the Foot Locker 3-Point Contest, part of NBA All-Star weekend at American Airlines Center on February 13, 2010.
COURTESY OF GETTY IMAGES

LeBron James #23 of the Cleveland Cavaliers talks to Kevin Garnett #5 after the Cavaliers' loss in Game 6 of the Eastern Conference Semifinals during the 2010 NBA Playoffs at TD Garden.
COURTESY OF GETTY IMAGES

Sending LeBron to Miami

THE CELTICS WERE not their regular dominant selves during the regular season in 2009–10, and many NBA observers speculated whether they would be unseated by the rising Cleveland Cavaliers and superstar LeBron James. James had taken his team to the finals in 2007 but fell short against the Celtics in 2008 and against the Orlando Magic in 2009. As an impending free agent, this could be potentially his last chance to reach the Finals with the Cavaliers (it wasn't, but that's another story). The favored Cavaliers ran into the fourth-seeded Celtics in the Eastern Conference semifinals, but the Celtics were playing their best basketball of the season. In one of the most impressive playoff performances by the Big Three, the Celtics sliced through the overwhelmed Cavaliers after dropping two of the first three games of the series. The Celtics evened the series behind a brilliant 29-point, 18-rebound, 13-assist performance from Rajon Rondo. In Game 5, the Celtics ran the Cavaliers off the floor, outscoring Cleveland 70–44 in the second half en route to a 120–88 win. Boston shot 55 percent, and Ray Allen led the club with 25 points and six 3-pointers. Game 6 would be more difficult, but the Celtics used a third-quarter run to take control with Rondo again showing his dazzling skills, scoring 21 points with 12 assists. After the final buzzer, with the Celtics advancing to the Eastern Conference Finals, James peeled off his jersey and walked disappointedly into the locker room. He signed with the Miami Heat a few weeks later.

Pierce Goes for 31 and 13 to Lead the Celtics Back to the Finals

THE 2009–10 CELTICS were not the regular season juggernaut of the previous two years. The team was aging, and coach Doc Rivers put more emphasis on health and less on regular-season wins. What's more, the Celtics entered the postseason as the fourth seed after a rather underwhelming 50–32 record. But Rivers accomplished his goal of ensuring his veteran players were fully healthy come playoff time. The run back to the finals was improbable. After besting Dwyane Wade and the Miami Heat in five games, the Celtics survived a rematch with the favored Cleveland Cavaliers and superstar LeBron James.

The Eastern Conference Finals was a rematch with the Orlando Magic, but with a healthy Garnett and the shooting of Paul Pierce and Ray Allen, the Celtics took a commanding 3–0 series lead. After Dwight Howard and the Magic won the next two games, Pierce closed out the series with one of his greatest playoff games as a Celtic. He scored 31 points with 13 rebounds as Boston finished off Orlando in six games. The Celtics won this series with balanced scoring, with four players averaging at least 10 points while Boston also shot 40 percent from the 3-point line. The Celtics needed to play their best basketball of the season to win this series, and they delivered. It was the second NBA Finals appearance in three years for the Big Three, and they again would face a familiar foe in the Los Angeles Lakers.

Paul Pierce reacts after scoring against the Orlando Magic in Game 6 of the Eastern Conference Finals during the 2010 NBA Playoffs at TD Garden.
COURTESY OF GETTY IMAGES

Big Baby Makes a Big Play

THE CELTICS WERE in trouble in the 2010 NBA Finals. They trailed 2 games to 1 after losing Game 3 at home, and they desperately needed a spark. Trailing at the start of the fourth quarter, third-year forward Glen "Big Baby" Davis, maligned at times by teammates and coaches for his conditioning issues and immaturity, responded in the biggest moment. Doc Rivers decided to look to his bench for a rally, and Davis and former Slam Dunk champion Nate Robinson teamed up to lead the Celtics to victory. Davis tied the game with a layup early in the fourth quarter and then gave the Celtics the lead for good on a layup assisted by Robinson. On one key play, Davis wrestled a rebound from the Lakers' Lamar Odom and scored a putback for a 70–64 lead, and he was fouled on the play. After making the layup, the burly Davis screamed in delight while the smaller Robinson leaped onto Davis's back in celebration. Davis scored nine of his 18 points in the final quarter, and the Celtics would even the series with a 96–89 win. Davis and Robinson combined for 30 points, and Davis added four key offensive rebounds as the desperate Celtics used their younger bench to pull out the win.

Glen Davis #11 and Nate Robinson react in the fourth quarter against the Los Angeles Lakers during Game 4 of the NBA Finals on June 10, 2010.
COURTESY OF GETTY IMAGES

Losing Game 7 of the 2010 Finals

BOSTON WON three of the first five games of the 2010 Finals against the Los Angeles Lakers and needed only one win in the final two games to capture its second crown in three years. But they lost Game 6 at Staples Center 89–67, and coach Doc Rivers would call it one of the more disappointing performances of his Celtics tenure. The Celtics now faced a winner-take-all game for the title. In what would be a game filled with drama, intrigue and back-and-forth play, Boston led the Lakers 57–53 in a defensive battle that was filled with missed shots and fouls. The Celtics needed to win one more quarter for the title, but they were exhausted from three consecutive deep playoff runs. Rasheed Wallace fouled out. Kendrick Perkins was out after tearing his anterior cruciate ligament in Game 6. Boston clung to a 64–61 lead with six minutes, 29 seconds left before Derek Fisher tied the game with a 3-pointer. The Lakers were erratic offensively, especially the great Kobe Bryant, but they did draw fouls and repeatedly reached the free throw line. Los Angeles attempted 14 free throws in the final six minutes, much to the chagrin of Celtics' players such as Kevin Garnett and Paul Pierce and coach Rivers. With the Celtics down 3 points and needing a defensive stop in the final minute, Wallace fouled Bryant with 25.7 seconds left. Bryant sank both. Despite a late Rajon Rondo 3-pointer, the championship dreams were over for the Celtics. They lost 83–79, a bitter defeat considering the Lakers attempted 37 free throws to the Celtics' 17, with Bryant and Pau Gasol combining for 28 attempts on their own. Rivers would later say that he would never get over the Game 7 loss, especially since it stymied the Celtics' chance at a dynasty. Boston would never reach another NBA Finals under Rivers, as the Big Three began to age and then were overtaken by LeBron James and the Miami Heat.

Rajon Rondo #9 drives the ball up court followed by the Los Angeles Lakers in Game 7 of the 2010 NBA Finals at the Staples Center.
COURTESY OF GETTY IMAGES

Celtics Sign Shaquille O'Neal

WITH KENDRICK PERKINS recovering from a torn ACL suffered during the NBA Finals, the Celtics needed another big man, and president of basketball operations Danny Ainge pursued one of the biggest during the following offseason. Shaquille O'Neal was beyond his prime, but he had accepted secondary roles in his previous stops in Cleveland and Phoenix and was looking to chase another championship. Ainge and O'Neal agreed to a one-year contract, giving the future Hall of Famer a chance to play with former rivals Kevin Garnett, Paul Pierce, and Ray Allen. O'Neal was 38 years old and not the physical force of a decade before. But he was still an imposing player and capable center. Unfortunately for the Celtics, they never got the best of O'Neal because of injury. After playing in 36 of the team's first 48 games, O'Neal suffered an Achilles injury that basically derailed the rest of his season. The Celtics were saving O'Neal for a potential playoff run and matchup against LeBron James and the Miami Heat. After sitting out 39 games, O'Neal returned for Game 3 of the Eastern Conference Semifinals against Miami and played eight minutes in a win. O'Neal came back and played four minutes in Game 4, but could barely run up and down the floor. That would be his last NBA game, and the Celtics lost the series in five games. The O'Neal experiment failed for Danny Ainge.

Shaquille O'Neal #36 and Kobe Bryant of the Lakers converse during their game at Staples Center on January 30, 2011.
COURTESY OF GETTY IMAGES

Ray Allen #20 shoots the record tying 3-point shot against Derek Fisher #2 of the Los Angeles Lakers on February 10, 2011 at TD Garden.
COURTESY OF GETTY IMAGES

Ray Allen Breaks 3-Point Record, February 10, 2011

RAY ALLEN ENTERED the NBA as a dynamic scorer with above-average athleticism. As his career progressed and the 3-point shot became more of a factor in the NBA game, he turned himself into one of the greatest shooters of all time. On a Thursday night at TD Garden, the Celtics hosted the Los Angeles Lakers for an NBA Finals rematch, but that was hardly the storyline. Allen needed just two 3-pointers to become the NBA's all-time leader. And with 1 minute, 48 seconds left in the first quarter, Allen took a fastbreak pass from Rajon Rondo, set his feet as he had done thousands of times, and released. The result: swish. It was the 2,561st 3-pointer of his illustrious career, breaking the record of all-time great Reggie Miller, who just happened to be calling the game for Turner Sports. TD Garden exploded after Allen's 3-pointer and after the first stoppage of play, Allen walked over to the broadcast booth courtside and hugged Miller, who happily handed the mantle of the greatest 3-point shooter to Allen. Of his 2,973 career 3-pointers, 798 were made over his five seasons in Boston. And it was one of the reasons why Allen was inducted into the Naismith Memorial Basketball Hall of Fame in 2018. Allen would hold his record until December 14, 2021, when Golden State Warriors sharpshooter Stephen Curry made his 2,974th in a win over the New York Knicks. Allen and Miller were each courtside to christen the new record-holder.

Celtics Place Four on the Eastern Conference All-Star Team in 2011

IF THERE WAS any question whether the Big Three was the Big Four, the 2011 All-Star Game was an indication. The Celtics sent their top four players to the spring classic in Los Angeles: Kevin Garnett, Paul Pierce, Ray Allen and Rajon Rondo. Rondo made his first All-Star appearance in Dallas in 2010. He emerged as one of the league's elite point guards during the late 2000s and his selection to the game came as no surprise. All four Celtics came off the bench as the West beat the East 148–143 with Kobe Bryant winning the MVP. Allen led the Celtics players with 12 points for the East. Rondo added eight assists in 20 minutes. It was the first time the Celtics had four players in the NBA All-Star Game since the 1961–62 season when Bill Russell, Bob Cousy, Sam Jones and Tom Heinsohn participated in the 1962 classic in St. Louis. Rondo would go on to be named to two more All-Star Games with the Celtics but 2011 was the only time the quartet would earn spots together.

Paul Pierce #34, Ray Allen #20, Rajon Rondo #9, and Kevin Garnett #5 of the Eastern Conference pose for a portrait prior to the 2011 NBA All-Star Game on February 20, at the Staples Center.

COURTESY OF GETTY IMAGES

Rondo Returns From Dislocated Elbow to Help Celtics in Playoffs

RAJON RONDO BECAME legendary for his toughness and grit during his years with the Celtics. He didn't back down from any challenge or any opponent. During Game 3 of the Eastern Conference Semifinals in 2011, Rondo faced one of his biggest obstacles when he got tangled with Miami's Dwyane Wade and suffered a dislocated elbow trying to break his fall. Rondo stayed on the floor for several moments before being helped into the locker room. Celtics team doctor Brian McKeon popped the elbow back into place and wrapped the area heavily. Rondo then checked back into the game to the delight of the sellout crowd at TD Garden. The Celtics went on to beat Wade, LeBron James, and the Heat 97–81. Rondo, despite intense pain, would go on to finish the series, which the Celtics lost in five games. Rondo averaged 10 points and 7.6 assists in the series, gaining the reputation as one of the toughest players in the NBA.

Rajon Rondo #9 dislocates his left elbow during a collision with Dwyane Wade #3 of the Miami Heat in Game 3 of the Eastern Conference Semifinals on May 7, 2011 at TD Garden.
COURTESY OF GETTY IMAGES

Celtics Edge 76ers to Advance to Eastern Conference Finals

IT WAS THE last deep playoff run of the Big Three with Kevin Garnett, Paul Pierce, and Ray Allen. They disposed of the Atlanta Hawks in the first round and were anticipating a juicy matchup with the top-seeded Chicago Bulls and MVP Derrick Rose. But Rose tore his ACL in the first-round series against the Philadelphia 76ers, and the Bulls lost to the upstart club. So it turned into a battle of old rivals, the experienced Celtics looking for one final run and the youthful 76ers looking to knock off the giant. The series was back and forth, with each team winning alternate games until the Game 7 matchup. In the finale, the wily veteran Celtics outlasted the 76ers in a rock fight, winning 85–75 behind 18 points apiece from Garnett and Rajon Rondo. The Celtics defense held the 76ers to 35 percent shooting and just 33 points in the first half. Garnett was the best player on the floor for the Celtics, averaging 19.7 points and 11 rebounds, while second-year guard Avery Bradley was critical for Doc Rivers in defending the Philadelphia backcourt of Jrue Holiday and Evan Turner.

Rajon Rondo #9 celebrates against the Philadelphia 76ers in Game 7 of the Eastern Conference Semifinals on May 26, 2012 at TD Garden.
COURTESY OF GETTY IMAGES

The Rajon Rondo Years

WHAT HAD BEEN an under-the-radar draft night trade in 2006 turned into a coup for Celtics president of basketball operations Danny Ainge. Rajon Rondo eventually became the floor leader in the third Big Three era, the young, brash point guard who had enough savvy and bravado to tell veterans Kevin Garnett, Paul Pierce, and Ray Allen where to be on the floor. Rondo played eight-plus seasons with the Celtics, finishing fourth all time in total assists and reaching the All-Star Game four times. Rondo became the fourth member of the Big Three, giving the Celtics a versatile and dominant lineup along with Kendrick Perkins. Rondo's unorthodox style made him unlike many other point guards of his era. A reluctant shooter, Rondo would much rather collect an assist than score a bucket, but he was a capable scorer when needed. And then there was playoff Rondo, who was able to step up big in the biggest games. In the 2010 Eastern Conference Semifinals against the favored Cleveland Cavaliers, Rondo led the Celtics to a major upset, averaging 20.7 points, 6.3 rebounds, and 11.8 assists in the six games. And in those most critical moments during the Big Three stretch, Rondo never left the floor, averaging more than 40 minutes per game in eight of his 15 playoff series with Boston. His most courageous moment occurred in 2011 during the Eastern Conference semifinal series against the Miami Heat, when he suffered a dislocated elbow in Game 3 but still played the rest of the series. Rondo had his critics and made some adversaries, but Celtics faithful could never dispute his desire to win and competitiveness.

Rajon Rondo #9 shoots against Gilbert Arenas #0 of the Washington Wizards at the Verizon Center on December 10, 2009 in Washington, D.C.
COURTESY OF GETTY IMAGES

Satch Sanders Inducted into Naismith Memorial Basketball Hall of Fame, 2011

TOM "SATCH" SANDERS has always been a model of class and dignity with the Celtics organization. He played 13 years in Boston as a defensive-minded forward, winning eight championships and checking the likes of Elgin Baylor and Bob Pettit on a nightly basis. While Sanders didn't put up the eye-popping statistics, he was an essential part of those title teams. After his playing career, Sanders was the first Black head coach at Harvard University (with former teammate K.C. Jones as his assistant coach) and then joined the Celtics staff as an assistant to Tom Heinsohn. But it was his work with the NBA that may have had the biggest impact. Sanders devised the NBA's Rookie Transition Program, a multi-day session that would introduce first-year players into the league, offering advice for how to handle the lifestyle, the money, and the other challenges of being a professional athlete. The transition program continues today, with former players and others speaking to rookies about the necessariy adjustments to procure a long career. Because of his many efforts in aiding the NBA, Sanders was inducted into the Naismith Memorial Basketball Hall of Fame as a contributor in 2011, a well-deserved honor for one of the great gentlemen of the game.

Inductee Tom "Satch" Sanders speaks to the audience during the Basketball Hall of Fame Enshrinement Ceremony on August 12, 2011 at Symphony Hall in Springfield, Massachusetts.
COURTESY OF GETTY IMAGES

Celtics Cancel Game Because of Marathon Bombings

THE BOSTON MARATHON is a wildly popular event in the city, with downtown shutting down on that third Monday in April as the marathoners take over. But on this tragic April day in 2013, Boston would be changed forever. Two bombs detonated near the finish line, killing three people and injuring many others. It was a dark day in the city's history, and there was fear across the area as the two perpetrators were on the run. Boston was in shock, and suddenly the Celtics' regular-season finale against the Indiana Pacers that evening carried little importance. The NBA and the Celtics made the astute decision to cancel the game and the team headed directly to its first-round playoff series with the New York Knicks. An emotional Doc Rivers told reporters that the game didn't matter and that he and the franchise were ready to help the city heal from the damage. A few days later Red Sox slugger David Ortiz made his impassioned speech prior to a home game at Fenway Park, galvanizing the fans by saying, "This is our (bleeping) city!"

Carlos Arredondo, who was among those who were aiding victims of the Boston Marathon bombing, on the court before the game between the Celtics and the New York Knicks during Game 4 of the Eastern Conference Quarterfinals on April 28, 2013 at TD Garden.

COURTESY OF GETTY IMAGES

Ainge Deals Pierce and Garnett to the Nets

IT WAS A difficult conversation for both men. Celtics president of basketball operations Danny Ainge and coach Doc Rivers discussed the future of the franchise after being eliminated in the first round of the 2013 playoffs by the New York Knicks. The Celtics were aging. Ray Allen had signed with the Miami Heat the year before, and Paul Pierce and Kevin Garnett were no longer in their primes. Rivers decided he did not want to be part of a rebuilding plan and accepted a job with the Los Angeles Clippers, while Ainge decided to completely rebuild, trading Pierce, Garnett, and Jason Terry to the Brooklyn Nets for a slew of draft picks and draft pick swaps. It ended a glorious era in Celtics basketball, a return to prosperity and a championship. But Ainge believed the Celtics should acquire assets for Pierce and Garnett instead of allowing them to age and the franchise to decline. The Celtics were three years removed from their last NBA Finals appearance and were trailing the Miami Heat and New York Knicks in the Eastern Conference. Pierce and Garnett finished as all-time great Celtics, and the trade was unpopular in Boston but understood by the fan base. Rivers once said the Big Three was a three-year plan, but it eventually lasted five years with one championship and one NBA Finals appearance. In the end, Ainge made the excruciating decision to move two cornerstones to secure the franchise's bright future. Even Pierce, a student of the game, said he understood the trade to a contender ready to win now.

Paul Pierce (right) and Kevin Garnett of the Brooklyn Nets interact during a press conference at the Barclays Center on July 18, 2013 in New York City.
COURTESY OF GETTY IMAGES

General manager Danny Ainge talks with Jayson Tatum during USA Basketball Men's National Team Training Camp at UCLA Health Training Center on August 13, 2019 in El Segundo, California.
COURTESY OF GETTY IMAGES

The Brilliance of "Trader" Danny Ainge

DANNY AINGE BECAME the Celtics' president of basketball operations in 2003, and he quickly gained a reputation for eagerly making trades to improve his roster. It wasn't that Ainge didn't believe in the draft, but he was always looking for the deal that would nab the next great Celtic. Ainge had a keen eye for talent, even for players who were considered flawed or under the radar. While his most popular deal during his tenure was acquiring Kevin Garnett and Ray Allen in separate deals during the summer of 2007—trades that helped the Celtics win a title—he also made a series of astute deals for players who blossomed in Boston. Ainge acquired a gangly University of Kentucky guard named Rajon Rondo on draft night in 2006, and Rondo eventually became the point guard and floor leader during the Big Three era. He made what was considered a minor, trade-deadline deal for an undersized guard named Isaiah Thomas from the Phoenix Suns, and Thomas turned in two of the more impressive seasons in team history, making the All-Star team twice. After the Celtics won the draft lottery in 2017, Ainge made the astute move of trading down to the third pick, knowing the Philadelphia 76ers had no intention of drafting Duke's Jayson Tatum. The 76ers drafted Washington guard Markelle Fultz while Ainge drafted Tatum and also received another first-round pick in the deal. He also had no hesitation in adding to the Celtics roster during playoff runs.

The Celtics introduce their new head coach, Brad Stevens, on July 5, 2013, at The Training Center at Healthpoint in Waltham, Massachusetts.
COURTESY OF GETTY IMAGES

Celtics Hire Brad Stevens as Coach

CELTICS PRESIDENT of Basketball Operations Danny Ainge was expected to search extensively for a new head coach in 2013. Doc Rivers decided he wanted no part of a rebuilding plan and accepted an offer to coach the Los Angeles Clippers. Ainge would need a coach ready for some difficult early seasons as the core of the championship team from a half decade ago was all gone. The search was expected to take most of the summer, but on a quiet July 3 afternoon, the Celtics sent out a press release announcing they had hired a coach. Brad Stevens, who led mid-major Butler to consecutive NCAA national championship games, was not on the list of projected candidates. But Ainge approached Stevens during Rivers's final season to gauge his interest in coming to the NBA ranks. Stevens was interested, and he became the NBA's youngest coach at 36, fully prepared for the rebuilding program. But the rebuilding didn't last long. Stevens had the Celtics back into the playoffs in his second season and led Boston to three Eastern Conference Finals appearances in his eight seasons. It was another Danny Ainge coup. He went the unconventional route and hired one of basketball's brightest minds when most basketball observers believed Stevens was destined to accept a coaching position at one of college basketball's bluebloods. Instead Stevens pursued his interest in the NBA, and Ainge got the desired leader of the franchise.

Hell Freezes Over: The Celtics Honor the Great Kobe Bryant

KOBE BRYANT WAS one of the NBA's all-time greats and played for the rival Lakers for 20 years. And while it took 12 years for Bryant to become a real part of the Lakers–Celtics rivalry, he played an important role in its resurrection when the two teams met in the 2008 and 2010 finals. Bryant decided to call it a career after the 2015–16 season, and in his farewell tour with the Lakers he visited TD Garden one final time on December 30, 2015. The Celtics welcomed him with open arms. The team's ownership brass along with president of basketball operations Danny Ainge presented Bryant with a piece of the Garden parquet floor that Bryant played on during the 2010 NBA Finals, a series the Lakers won in seven games. Bryant was given a standing ovation when he was announced during pre-game introductions, and the Lakers, who entered the matchup with a 5–27 record, beat the Celtics 112–104. It was Bryant's final game in Boston, and he scored 15 points with 11 rebounds to help the effort. Bryant tragically passed away in January 2020.

Kobe Bryant #24 of the Los Angeles Lakers after the game against the Boston Celtics on December 30, 2015 at TD Garden.
COURTESY OF GETTY IMAGES

Celtics Sign Al Horford

FOR DECADES THERE had been the perception that Boston could not attract major free agents, especially players of color. The city had an undeserved reputation as a difficult place to play and live for players of color, and that reputation impacted the Celtics' ability to sign major free agents for two decades. All of their great players during that stretch were acquired via the draft or trade. That was until Al Horford listened to the Celtics' pitch. Horford became a free agent in 2016 after nine years with the Atlanta Hawks, and the Celtics scraped up enough salary cap space to offer the forward/center a maximum contract. On the day free agency began, Horford accepted the Boston offer, posting on his social media page that he was becoming a Celtic. It was a sign of change for the Boston franchise. All-Star players such as Gordon Hayward and Kemba Walker would follow Horford to Boston as free agents. Horford was the model of stability the Celtics needed, and he stepped in as a team leader and role model for the young roster. Horford played three seasons in his first stint with the Celtics, reaching one All-Star Game and helping Boston to two Eastern Conference Finals. He returned to Boston via trade in 2021 and helped the Celtics to the NBA Finals before signing a two-year extension, showing his love and dedication to Boston. The 38-year-old Horford was a key contributor on the 2024 title team, the first championship in his 17-year career.

Al Horford poses for a portrait during the Boston Celtics Media Day at TD Garden on September 26, 2016.
COURTESY OF GETTY IMAGES

The Drafting of Jaylen Brown

AS PART OF the trade that sent Kevin Garnett and Paul Pierce to the Brooklyn Nets, the Celtics received the third overall pick in the 2016 draft. The Celtics had their choice of top talent such as international prospect Dragan Bender, Providence guard Kris Dunn, and Oklahoma sharpshooter Buddy Hield. Instead, the Celtics opted for a player unknown to most local fans, a hard-driving, athletic guard/forward named Jaylen Brown out of California. During the Celtics' draft party, boos could be heard after the announcement of Brown was made. Those fans would soon regret those jeers. Brown has turned into a franchise cornerstone, earning three All-Star Game appearances and averaging 18.6 points in his first eight seasons in Boston. Brown helped the Celtics to four Eastern Conference Finals, the 2022 NBA Finals and he was stellar in Boston's 2024 playoff run, winning MVP of the Eastern Conference Finals and the NBA Finals, helping capture its 18th championship. Brown has earned a reputation as a tough player who has worked feverishly to improve his game over the years. He has become a better midrange and 3-point shooter and has always been able to get to the rim and high in the air with his athleticism. Brown is also one of seven Celtics to have scored at least 50 points in a regular-season game, tallying 50 in a January 2, 2022, win over the Orlando Magic. And he became only the second Celtics player with at least 10 3-pointers in game when he canned 10 in a March 21, 2021, win over the Magic. Brown has also made an impact off the floor with his charity and community work and through his membership in the NBA Players Association.

Jaylen Brown #7 dunks against the Dallas Mavericks on November 16, 2016 at TD Garden.
COURTESY OF GETTY IMAGES

Isaiah Thomas Drops 52 on the Miami Heat, December 30, 2016

ISAIAH THOMAS COLLECTED a plethora of amazing moments in his 179 games with the Celtics, many of which were scoring binges that carried Boston to victories. On a late December night in 2016, Thomas was brilliant in leading the Celtics to a 117–114 victory over the Miami Heat. Thomas scored a career-high 52 points, the seventh-most points by a Celtic, on 15-for-26 shooting, including nine 3-pointers. Thomas was a prolific scorer despite his 5-foot, 9-inch frame, and he thrilled Celtics fans with his ability to score over much larger players. Thomas was fearless, always willing to take the big shot, such as in the final minute against the Heat. With the Celtics clinging to a 108–106 lead with 37 seconds left, Thomas drained a clinching 30-footer for his 50th point. He added two free throws to become the fifth Celtic to score 50 points in a game, following Larry Bird, Kevin McHale, Sam Jones and Paul Pierce.

Isaiah Thomas celebrates after scoring against the Miami Heat on March 26, 2017 at TD Garden.
COURTESY OF GETTY IMAGES

Paul Pierce Hits His Final Shot at TD Garden

THE CELTICS WANTED to rebuild, and Paul Pierce was an aging star looking for one final championship run. President of basketball operations Danny Ainge traded Pierce and Kevin Garnett to the Brooklyn Nets in 2013. Pierce would play one season for the Nets and then sign with the Washington Wizards, where he played for one season. He made emotional returns to Boston with the Nets and Wizards, but he announced that the 2016–2017 season with the Los Angeles Clippers and former coach Doc Rivers would be his last in the NBA. At age 39, Pierce was no longer a regular contributor, but Rivers made the class move of giving Pierce the start in his final game in Boston. He played the first four minutes and 57 seconds before spending the next 42-plus minutes on the bench. With the game already decided, Rivers summoned Pierce for the final 20 seconds as the TD Garden crowd chanted his name. Pierce walked onto the floor for the Clippers' final possession and launched a 3-pointer from well behind the line at the top of the key. Swish. PA announcer Eddie Palladino screamed, "Paul Pierce for three!!!" in his home cadence. A humbled Pierce jogged down the floor as time expired, waving goodbye to the fans and appreciating their support. "The fans are great fans. They were truly able to appreciate what I've been able to do for this franchise. I really feel the love and I'm thankful to come in here one last time."

Paul Pierce #34 of the LA Clippers handles the ball against the Celtics on February 5, 2017 at TD Garden.
COURTESY OF GETTY IMAGES

Isaiah Thomas Goes Down in the Eastern Conference Finals, 2017

ISAIAH THOMAS BECAME more than a reliable scorer when he was acquired by the Celtics in 2015; he became a leader, All-Star, and franchise cornerstone. And in one of the more productive seasons in club history, Thomas finished third in the NBA in scoring at 28.9 points per game, the second-best average by a Celtic ever. He was essential to the Celtics' success in the playoffs, but as the team approached the postseason, Thomas was battling a hip issue that limited his production. Still, Thomas led Boston to a comeback against the eighth-seeded Chicago Bulls to win in six and then a stellar performance against the Washington Wizards. Thomas tallied 53 points in the Celtics' Game 2 win and led Boston with 29 in the Game 7 win. All the while, Thomas was playing with a torn muscle in his right hip. It finally caught up with him in the Eastern Conference Finals matchup with the Cleveland Cavaliers. After scoring 17 points in the Game 1 loss, a hobbled Thomas could only log 17 minutes of Game 2 before leaving with hip pain. That would be the final appearance of the series and his final game as a Celtic. Thomas was traded to the Cleveland Cavaliers in the offseason, ending his sparkling run with the Celtics. Boston would lose the Cleveland series in five games, unable to compete without Thomas.

Isaiah Thomas of the Cleveland Cavaliers during a game against the Celtics on October 17, 2017 at Quicken Loans Arena in Cleveland, Ohio.
COURTESY OF GETTY IMAGES

Playing Through the Worst Pain: Isaiah Thomas

NOT ONLY DID Isaiah Thomas put his body on the line during his two-and-a-half years with the Celtics, but he also played with a heavy heart during a pivotal time in franchise history. The Celtics had championship aspirations in 2017, finishing as the number one seed in the Eastern Conference, led by Thomas's scoring brilliance. A day before the Celtics opened the playoffs against the eighth-seeded Chicago Bulls, Thomas found out that his sister Chyna, 22, had passed away in a one-car accident returning home from work in Thomas's native Tacoma. Thomas was devastated, crying in the arms of teammate Avery Bradley, a friend since their prep days in Washington, during a pre-game workout. Thomas played through that Chicago series grief-stricken, but he was able to lift the Celtics to a series win despite losing the first two games. Thomas made the valiant move of stepping away from the team to attend his sister's funeral without missing a playoff game. He left the team immediately after they closed out the Bulls in Chicago and returned to Boston just before Game 1 of the Eastern Conference semifinals series against the Washington Wizards. Thomas was brilliant in that series despite his heavy heart, and he became wildly popular amongst the Celtics fan base for his bravery and perseverance.

Isaiah Thomas reacts during Game 1 of the Eastern Conference Semifinals against the Washington Wizards at TD Garden on April 30, 2017. Thomas lost his front tooth after colliding with Otto Porter Jr.
COURTESY OF GETTY IMAGES

The Kelly Olynyk Game

KELLY OLYNYK WAS drafted in 2013 as a skilled big man, a stretch four who could shoot from the perimeter and also defend and score in the post. And while he experienced an uneven four seasons in Boston, he shined when the Celtics needed him most in Game 7 of the 2017 Eastern Conference semifinals against the Washington Wizards. The top-seeded Celtics were pushed to the brink by John Wall, Bradley Beal, and the rising Wizards. While Isaiah Thomas had carried the team throughout the playoffs, it needed a lift in this deciding game. Olynyk was ready for this moment. Coming off the bench, Olynyk scored 26 points in 28 minutes, including 14 in the fourth quarter as the Celtics sealed a 115–105 win. The Wizards cut a 13-point deficit to four with five minutes and 54 seconds left before Olynyk took over. He responded with a pair of layups and then a mammoth 3-pointer for a 10-point lead on an assist from Thomas. That dagger put away the Wizards and sent the Celtics to the Eastern Conference Finals against the Cleveland Cavaliers. It would also be the finest moment in Boston for Olynyk, who signed with the Miami Heat a few weeks later after the Celtics renounced his rights to sign Gordon Hayward. Olynyk still receives ovations each time he returns to TD Garden, primarily because of that game.

Kelly Olynyk celebrates during Game 7 of the Eastern Conference Semifinals against the Washington Wizards on May 15, 2017 at TD Garden.
COURTESY OF GETTY IMAGES

The Drafting of Jayson Tatum

CELTICS PRESIDENT OF basketball operations Danny Ainge knew who he wanted all along going into the 2017 draft, and he knew the Philadelphia 76ers didn't feel as strongly as he did about Duke forward Jayson Tatum. So instead of taking Tatum with the No. 1 overall pick, Ainge traded down to the third pick with the 76ers, knowing they were interested in Washington guard Markelle Fultz. So not only did Ainge walk away with the best player in the draft, he also acquired a future first-round pick. The drafting of Tatum changed the course of the Celtics franchise. After a strong season at Duke, Tatum was NBA ready, drawing comparisons to Paul Pierce with his offensive prowess at an early age, and he played with a fearlessness and savvy well beyond his years. Tatum has turned into one of the NBA's elite players, reaching the All-Star Game five times, being named first-team All-NBA three times and also the Eastern Conference Finals Most Valuable Player in leading the Celtics to the 2022 NBA Finals. Tatum also became the second Celtic to score 60 points in a game (joining Larry Bird) when he dropped 60 in an overtime win over the San Antonio Spurs on April 30, 2021. Tatum's finest moment may have occurred on May 13, 2022, when he carried the Celtics to a Game 6 win over the Milwaukee Bucks in the Eastern Conference semifinals with 46 points on the road. It was a must-win game for the Celtics, and Tatum was brilliant. He has had many brilliant nights as a Celtic and is on his way to being an all-time franchise great. And Tatum was an essential part of the Celtics' first championship in 16 years.

Jayson Tatum poses for a portrait after being drafted number three overall by the Celtics during the NBA Draft on June 22, 2017.

COURTESY OF GETTY IMAGES

Celtics Acquire Kyrie Irving, Sign Gordon Hayward in the Summer of 2017

COMING OFF A stunning run to the Eastern Conference Finals behind rising star Jaylen Brown and veteran Al Horford, Celtics president of basketball operations Danny Ainge chased two All-Stars that could take his franchise to the next level. A few days into free agency, Ainge was able to procure Utah forward Gordon Hayward, who had played for Celtics coach Brad Stevens at Butler. It was the team's second major free-agent signing in two years, the team having signed Atlanta's Al Horford the previous summer. Hayward chose the Celtics over re-signing with the Jazz and declined offers from the Miami Heat and Charlotte Hornets. Hayward was projected as the team's small forward for the next several years, a premium scorer just entering his prime. Six weeks later, Ainge then made the controversial trade of sending popular but injured guard Isaiah Thomas, forward Jae Crowder, and recent first-round pick Ante Zizic to the Cleveland Cavaliers for brilliant guard and NBA champion Kyrie Irving. Thomas was a two-time All-Star during two-and-a-half years in Boston and played through his sister's tragic passing and a painful hip injury. Irving, however, was expected to upgrade the position because of his ability to score and distribute. Irving had requested a trade from the Cavaliers and was delighted to come to Boston, where his father had played college basketball at Boston University. Hayward was reunited with his college coach and was coming off his first All-Star appearance. The acquisitions were a sign the Celtics were prepared to compete with the elite teams in the NBA.

Kyrie Irving #11 and Gordon Hayward are introduced as the newest members of the Celtics at TD Garden on September 1, 2017 in Boston.
COURTESY OF GETTY IMAGES

Gordon Hayward Suffers Ghastly Injury

EXPECTATIONS WERE SO high for the Celtics in 2017–18. They were fully loaded with Kyrie Irving, Gordon Hayward, Jaylen Brown, Jayson Tatum, and Al Horford. They began the season in Cleveland against the defending Eastern Conference champion Cavaliers. But that momentum and excitement dissipated quickly. Hayward leaped for an alley-oop five minutes into the game and landed awkwardly, with his full weight putting pressure on his left leg. In one of the ugliest injuries in sports history, Hayward lay on the floor at Quicken Loans Arena with his left leg pointing in an unnatural direction. Cleveland guard Dwyane Wade and several players on the Cavaliers bench turned their heads in horror as Hayward waited for a stretcher. He was carried off the floor. Celtics forward Semi Ojeleye gathered the team for a prayer. Marcus Smart hugged an inconsolable Irving, and the game hardly mattered. Hayward suffered a broken tibia and dislocated ankle and would miss the rest of the season. It was an injury for which Hayward would never fully recover from in Boston. A player who had such high expectations as a free agent would never fulfill that promise as a Celtic. Hayward would return the next season and continue his career, but he was never quite the same player. It was a devastating injury that impacted the franchise.

Kyrie Irving #11 consoles Gordon Hayward #20 after Hayward was injured while playing the Cleveland Cavaliers at Quicken Loans Arena on October 17, 2017 in Cleveland.
COURTESY OF GETTY IMAGES

Celtics Go on 16-Game Winning Streak Without Hayward

Kyrie Irving #11 handles the ball against the San Antonio Spurs on October 30, 2017 at TD Garden in Boston.

COURTESY OF GETTY IMAGES

THE CELTICS WERE reeling after losing Gordon Hayward to a scary leg injury on opening night. They dropped that game to the Cleveland Cavaliers and then the home opener against the Milwaukee Bucks. Boston looked like a shell-shocked team that would struggle in the early season. That wasn't the case. After that loss to Milwaukee, the Celtics, led by Kyrie Irving, Jayson Tatum, Jaylen Brown, and Al Horford, went on a 16-game winning streak, tied for the fourth-longest in franchise history. A team that was devastated by Hayward's injury galvanized and were dominant for a two-month period, collecting wins over the 76ers, Heat, and Bucks; sweeping a road trip at Oklahoma City, Orlando, and Atlanta; and topping the rival Los Angeles Lakers at home. The 16th win came in overtime against the Dallas Mavericks, when Irving went for 47 points. The Celtics proved they could not only contend in the Eastern Conference but win the Eastern Conference without Hayward. The streak would end in Miami, when a valiant Celtics rally fell short. Boston found out during the run that Tatum would be a major contributor in his first season and that Brown was ready to step in for Hayward.

Celtics Retire Pierce's Jersey on February 11, 2018

PAUL PIERCE PLAYED 15 years in the Celtics green, becoming the team's second all-time leading scorer behind the great John Havlicek. Less than a year after his retirement from the Los Angeles Clippers, the Celtics retired Pierce's No. 34 in an emotional ceremony at TD Garden. Donning a green plaid jacket, Pierce was given a standing ovation and gave an emotional and spirited speech with his family, Celtics legends, former teammates, and current Celtics looking on. Kevin Garnett, Doc Rivers, Rajon Rondo, and Kendrick Perkins all watched as Pierce's number was raised to the rafters. It capped an improbable and amazing career for the Los Angeles native who grew up minutes from the Inglewood Forum as a fan of the Los Angeles Lakers. He slipped to the 10th overall pick in the 1998 draft, right into the Celtics' hands, and he eventually became a franchise cornerstone, big-game player, and NBA champion. Pierce is the Celtics' all-time leader in 3-point field goals and steals, and he ranks third in games played and seventh in total rebounds. "If I never make the Hall of Fame," Pierce told the audience, "to go up as a Celtic, my number here, that's probably all I could ever ask for. That will be enough for me. There's no fans like Boston. There's no organization like this. This is a first-class organization." Pierce would get his Hall of Fame wish, however, being inducted into the Naismith Memorial Basketball Hall of Fame in 2021.

Paul Pierce and his son, Prince raise his number during the Celtics' retirement ceremony after playing the Cleveland Cavaliers at TD Garden in Boston on February 11, 2018.
COURTESY OF GETTY IMAGES

Jayson Tatum Dunks on LeBron, May 28, 2018

JAYSON TATUM WAS a major prep prospect coming out of St. Louis, and he was able to attend the basketball camps of some of his idols, including Kevin Durant and LeBron James. What's more, there's a photo of a pre-teen Tatum with James from the mid-2000s. James was one of Tatum's basketball idols. During his rookie season, Tatum helped the Celtics reach the Eastern Conference Finals despite season-ending injuries to Gordon Hayward and Kyrie Irving. These young Celtics were brash and fearless, ready to take on all opponents in what was considered an improbable run to the NBA Finals. They matched up with the savvy and championship-pedigreed Cleveland Cavaliers in the conference finals. In the pivotal Game 7 the Celtics were trailing 71–67 with six minutes, 41 seconds left when a 20-year-old Tatum drove in the middle of the lane and saw a 33-year-old James waiting there. Without hesitation, the baby-faced Tatum reared back for a one-handed hammer dunk, catching James leaning back. The thunderous dunk sent the TD Garden crowd into delirium and Tatum chest-bumped James as a sign of respect, young buck dunking on grizzled veteran. It was one of the first of many dazzling playoff moments for Tatum, the Celtics' first-round draft pick in 2017. Although he was a rookie at the time, Tatum carried the Celtics to the brink of the Finals like a seasoned pro, averaging 17.9 points on nearly 50 percent shooting, and of course, that famous dunk.

Jayson Tatum #0 dunks the ball against LeBron James #23 of the Cleveland Cavaliers during Game 7 of the Eastern Conference Finals on May 27, 2018 at TD Garden.
COURTESY OF GETTY IMAGES

Falling Short in Game 7 to LeBron and the Cavaliers

THE 2017–18 CELTICS were on the verge of dethroning the three-time defending Eastern Conference champions. They played well enough without Gordon Hayward and Kyrie Irving to earn a three-games-to-two series lead behind the young duo of Jayson Tatum and Jaylen Brown and the veteran savvy of Al Horford. After losing Game 6 in Cleveland, the Celtics needed just one home win to reach their first NBA Finals in eight years. But that would be a difficult task against the great LeBron James and the battle-hardened Cavaliers. Game 7 was a rock fight with both defenses dominating, and the team that would gather the most offensive momentum would prevail. The Celtics had relied heavily on the 3-pointer, and that was the case again in Game 7. But the Celtics could not consistently hit the long-range shot, missing 15 of 19 attempts in the first half. Still, they led 43–39. In the third quarter, Boston scored just 13 points, missing 15 of its 20 shot attempts and all seven 3-point attempts. The Celtics desperately needed a spark in the fourth quarter and led 64–61 after a Marcus Morris 3-pointer, but they would then go nearly four minutes without scoring a field goal. Not even a thundering Tatum dunk on James could ignite the Celtics offensively. The Cavaliers lumbered to an 87–79 win and celebrated the conference title on the TD Garden floor. Boston missed 32 of 39 3-point attempts and shot 34.1 percent overall. A couple of more baskets would have fueled the Celtics to the finals. Instead, they were dealt a crushing loss.

Jayson Tatum #0 reacts as he stands next to LeBron James of the Cleveland Cavaliers in the second half during Game Seven of the 2018 NBA Eastern Conference Finals at TD Garden on May 27, 2018.
COURTESY OF GETTY IMAGES

Celtics Beat Bulls by a Record 56 Points, December 8, 2018

THE CELTICS RODE into Chicago on a four-game winning streak against the struggling Bulls and destroyed Chicago 133–77 on December 8, 2018. The Celtics did not have a player score more than 23 points but had eight players score in double figures. Third-year forward Jaylen Brown led the Celtics with 23 points off the bench while Daniel Theis added 22 points and 10 rebounds. Theis was an incredible plus-50 in his 32 minutes. It was the largest margin of victory in the 50-year history of the Celtics, besting a 51-point win over the Philadelphia Warriors in 1962. The Celtics scored the game's first 17 points and then never trailed, outscoring the Bulls 69–34 in the second half. Second-year forward Jayson Tatum added 18 points for the Celtics while Terry Rozier scored 15. The Celtics shot nearly 54 percent from the field and blitzed the Bulls with 22 3-pointers. It was also the worst loss in Bulls history, and it came in the third game coaching for interim coach Jim Boylen, who had taken over for the fired Fred Hoiberg. In their five-game winning streak, the Celtics outscored opponents by nearly 30 points per game, and the win over the Bulls was one of the most impressive performances of the season.

Terry Rozier #12 shoots the ball against the Chicago Bulls on December 8, 2018 at the United Center in Chicago.
COURTESY OF GETTY IMAGES

Jayson Tatum Wins 2019 Skills Challenge with Halfcourt Shot

THE CELTICS ACTUALLY won the NBA's Draft Lottery in 2017 after years of bad luck with the process, and shrewd general manager Danny Ainge was able to swap picks with the Philadelphia 76ers and draft gifted Duke forward Jayson Tatum with the third pick. On the road to Tatum's development into a superstar, he was invited to the Rising Stars Challenge at All-Star Weekend for standout first- and second-year players, giving him the opportunity to show his versatility by participating in the 2019 Skills Challenge in Charlotte. Tatum advanced to the Final Round against Atlanta sharpshooter Trae Young. Young appeared on his way to a victory by racing the ball down the floor far ahead of Tatum to score the winning basket. But Tatum pulled up from halfcourt and banked in the winner as Young's 3-point attempt missed. Tatum simply raised his arms in victory as the stunned crowd cheered vigorously. Tatum had beaten Memphis's Mike Conley and Denver's Nikola Jokic to advance to the final. Tatum would eventually become a staple at All-Star Weekend as a Sunday game participant. He attempted to defend his Skills Challenge title in 2020 but lost to close buddy Bam Adebayo of the Miami Heat.

Jayson Tatum celebrates with the trophy after winning the Taco Bell Skills Challenge as part of the NBA All-Star Weekend at Spectrum Center on February 16, 2019 in Charlotte, North Carolina.
COURTESY OF GETTY IMAGES

Marcus Smart Makes 11 Threes in a Game, January 18, 2020

MARCUS SMART HAS always loved the 3-point shot, but the 3-point shot hasn't always loved Marcus Smart. While he works feverishly at the long-range shots, he has earned a reputation as a streaky shooter. Smart has shot the Celtics into games but also out of games. On January 18, 2020, he was unstoppable from beyond the arc. Smart hit a career-high 11 3-pointers, breaking a team record in a 123–119 loss to the Phoenix Suns. Smart scored 37 points and was 11 for 22 from the 3-point line in keeping the Celtics close all evening. He drained six 3-pointers in the first half, added another in the third, and then tried to rally Boston against Devin Booker and the Suns with four threes in the fourth period. It was a career night for Smart, who would not hit more than six 3-pointers at any other point during the 2019–20 season. Smart's 3-point shooting has always been a point of contention amongst Celtics fans because of his inconsistency, but he was brilliant on this night.

Marcus Smart #36 shoots during a game against the Phoenix Suns on January 18, 2020 at TD Garden.
COURTESY OF GETTY IMAGES

Celtics Represent in the Bubble

THE CELTICS WERE preparing for a difficult road game at Milwaukee scheduled for March 12, 2020 when the world was suddenly overwhelmed by a crisis. Utah's Rudy Gobert became the first NBA player to test positive for COVID-19, and the NBA made the stunning decision to postpone the 2019–20 season. The NBA, like all other professional sports leagues in America, was dormant for nearly five months until play resumed under controlled conditions. The Celtics were one of 22 teams selected to play in the NBA bubble, a campus-like environment where games would resume with no fans, and where players, coaches, executives, and media would be tested for the coronavirus daily. All teams would stay at selected hotels at Disneyworld in Orlando, Florida, and play regular season and playoff games at three arenas on the Disney campus. The Celtics would play eight regular season games and then continue with a playoff tournament and then finally the NBA Finals. The Celtics finished the regular season in the NBA Bubble as the number three seed with a 48–24 record (the season was abbreviated by 10 games). They advanced to the Eastern Conference Finals before losing to the Miami Heat.

Paul George #13 of the L.A. Clippers shoots against the Denver Nuggets during Game 7 of the Western Conference Semifinals on September 13, 2020 in Orlando, Florida at the AdventHealth Arena.

COURTESY OF GETTY IMAGES

Celtics Edge Raptors in Epic 7-Game Series in the Bubble

DESPITE THE NBA season being moved to Orlando because of the pandemic, the Celtics faced familiar foes in the postseason, matching up with the Philadelphia 76ers in the first round and easily disposing of their Atlantic Division rivals. The next series wouldn't be so easy, even though it started out that way. The Celtics appeared determined to take care of business against the Toronto Raptors, winning Game 1 in a blowout and Game 2 behind a 34-point performance from Jayson Tatum. The Celtics were eerily close to taking Game 3, needing just one defensive stop to take a stranglehold on the series. A defensive miscue on coverage allowed Toronto's OG Anunoby to get open for a three, and he drained the winning shot at the buzzer, changing the series. Toronto won the next game behind 23 points from Pascal Siakam. Jaylen Brown and Kemba Walker then combined for 48 points to help Boston easily win Game 5 before the Raptors won Game 6 in double overtime. Game 7 was an epic struggle, with both defenses dominating, and the game came down to a few key plays. The Celtics began the fourth quarter with a critical 7–0 run to take an 8-point lead, which included a 3-pointer from Walker. The Raptors battled back, cutting the Celtics' lead to two points with one minute left. After Tatum sank a free throw, forward Grant Williams partially blocked a potential tying 3-pointer from sharpshooter Fred VanVleet and Brown gathered the rebound. Walker sank the clinching free throws, and the Celtics were on their way to the Eastern Conference Finals.

Kemba Walker drives against the Toronto Raptors during Game 3 of the Eastern Conference Semifinals on September 7, 2020 at the The Field House at ESPN Wide World of Sports Complex in Orlando, Florida.
COURTESY OF GETTY IMAGES

Celtics Lose Painful Series to Miami Heat in the Bubble

THE CELTICS WATCHED the playoff tournament in the bubble turn their way. The top-seeded Milwaukee Bucks had been eliminated by the fifth-seeded Miami Heat. The Celtics then topped the second-seeded Toronto Raptors, making them the favorites against the Heat to reach the finals for the first time in 10 years. The Miami series was one of the low points in the Brad Stevens coaching era. The Celtics blew a big lead in Game 1 and lost in overtime when Jayson Tatum's dunk attempt was blocked by Miami's Bam Adebayo. The Heat then rallied to win Game 2, prompting a major post-game locker-room argument that caused a rift between Marcus Smart and Jaylen Brown. Boston would come back to take Game 3, but then would allow Miami rookie Tyler Herro to score 37 points in a decisive Game 4 win. Tatum's 31 points led Boston in Game 5, but the Celtics couldn't generate enough momentum or clutch plays in the fourth quarter to fight off Miami, losing Game 6 and the series. It was a crushing loss for the Celtics, who believed they had the roster with Kemba Walker, Tatum, Brown, and Gordon Hayward to make an NBA Finals run. Miami was the tougher team and made the winning plays down the stretch. It was a difficult reality for Celtics faithful to digest.

Jayson Tatum #0 and Daniel Theis react after their win over the Miami Heat in Game 5 of the Eastern Conference Finals during the NBA Playoffs at AdventHealth Arena at the ESPN Wide World of Sports Complex on September 25, 2020 in Orlando, Florida.
COURTESY OF GETTY IMAGES

The Passing of Tom Heinsohn

TOM HEINSOHN WAS not only a Hall of Fame player and coach but a Celtics television analyst for nearly 40 years, teaming with Mike Gorman on local telecasts beginning in 1981, a few years after his coaching career ended. Heinsohn became a staple for Celtics telecasts, providing lively commentary while ripping officials for bad calls and giving his pro-Celtics take. Players who made hustle plays earned what were called "Tommy points," and he would give some of the players endearing nicknames such as "The Little Guy" for Isaiah Thomas or "Waltaa!" for forward Walter McCarty. Heinsohn also worked for CBS during its NBA telecasts during the 1980s and '90s and teamed with Dick Stockton to call all three Celtics–Lakers NBA Finals matchups and also many of the league's other big games during that era. For a new generation of Celtics fans, Heinsohn became one of the voices of the team, becoming wildly popular for his berating of officials during telecasts. Heinsohn remained in the booth until shortly before his death in November 2020 at age 86.

Bill Russell and Tommy Heinsohn watch the game between the Celtics and the Orlando Magic in Game 2 of the Eastern Conference Semifinals during the NBA Playoffs at TD Banknorth Garden on May 6, 2009.
COURTESY OF GETTY IMAGES

Brown, Tatum Named to All-Star Game in Atlanta

THE DUO OF Jayson Tatum and Jaylen Brown came to Boston a year apart, and the two have been linked because of their similar talents and both being drafted third overall. While there have been questions about their ability to play together, their talent is unquestioned. Both got off to brilliant starts in the 2020–21 season, and each was named to the NBA's All-Star Game in Atlanta in March 2021. The original All-Star Game scheduled for Indiana was canceled and moved to Atlanta in a controlled environment with limited attendance at State Farm Arena. For Brown, it was a chance to play in an All-Star Game near his hometown of Marietta, Georgia. For Tatum, it was a chance to establish himself as a perennial All-Star, playing in his second game. Both players entered the 3-Point Contest. Brown and Tatum were on different teams as the NBA went to a draft instead of the previous conference format. Brown was chosen by team captain LeBron James, and Tatum was a selection of team captain Kevin Durant. Brown played 26 minutes and scored 22 points for the victorious Team LeBron while Tatum, who started for Team Durant, added 21 points in 17 minutes. Celtics faithful hoped that the Tatum–Brown All-Star pairing was a sign of things to come in Boston.

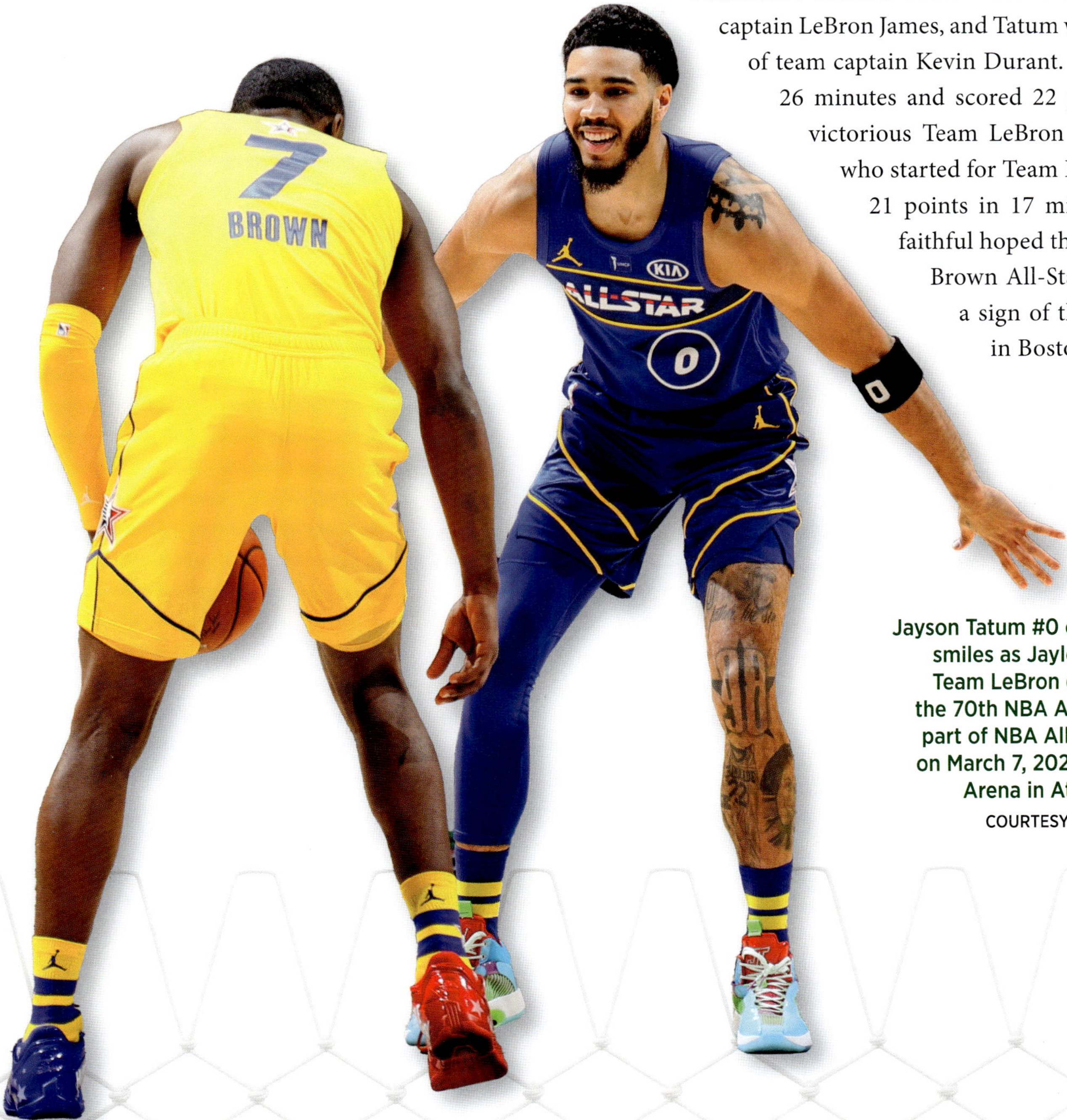

Jayson Tatum #0 of Team Durant smiles as Jaylen Brown #7 of Team LeBron dribbles during the 70th NBA All Star Game as part of NBA All-Star Weekend on March 7, 2021 at State Farm Arena in Atlanta, Georgia.
COURTESY OF GETTY IMAGES

April 30, 2021: Jayson Tatum Drops 60

THE NIGHT DIDN'T look promising for the Celtics and seemed especially unlikely to become the platform for one of the most outstanding offensive performances in team history. The Celtics trailed the San Antonio Spurs 79–48 at halftime, and boos were raining down on the floor at TD Garden. The only positive was Jayson Tatum, who had scored half of the Celtics' points and made nine of their 16 field goals. The second half was a different story: Tatum continued to score, but his teammates helped out and the defense began getting stops. The Celtics rallied furiously, and Tatum scored 21 points in the fourth quarter to give him 50. The Spurs made some late free throws to force overtime, with Tatum missing a potential game-winning jumper at the buzzer. He would soon atone for that miss, scoring 10 points in the overtime period, including the final four free throws for 60 points and a 143–140 win. Tatum became the second Celtic (joining Larry Bird) to record 60 points in a game, tying the franchise record. He made 20 of his 37 shots and 15 of 17 free throws with eight rebounds and no turnovers in 45 minutes. It was a masterful performance from Tatum and one that was desperately needed. The Celtics trailed by as many as 32 points, and they jumped on Tatum's back to capture the improbable win. Tatum was unstoppable on that evening, as his ascension toward being one of the great Celtics of all time continued.

Jayson Tatum #0 shoots the ball against the San Antonio Spurs on April 30, 2021 at TD Garden.
COURTESY OF GETTY IMAGES

Celtics Retire Garnett's Jersey

HE PLAYED JUST six seasons in Boston but left with a championship and an NBA Finals appearance and helped change the culture of the Boston franchise. Kevin Garnett came to Boston after 12 years with the Minnesota Timberwolves, but most of his team accomplishments came with the Celtics. The organization rewarded him by retiring his No. 5 in March 2022. Garnett was named the 2008 Defensive Player of the Year in his first season in Boston, but more importantly, he fostered the Celtics return to respectability after 22 years without an NBA championship. Boston was a losing, downtrodden franchise when Garnett was acquired from Minnesota in the summer of 2007. His passion for the game, determination to win, and leadership ability soon brought the Celtics back into championship contention. The Celtics haven't returned to those losing ways since, and Garnett can be credited as one of the most impactful players in franchise history. And, of course, during his acceptance speech in front of a packed TD Garden, Garnett dropped a couple of expletives and was greeted by several former teammates, including Ray Allen, who made a surprise appearance. Allen and Garnett feuded after Allen signed with the rival Miami Heat after the 2011–12 season, and the two had spoken little over the next decade. Garnett's jersey retirement allowed the Big Three to come together once again, much to the delight of the crowd and many former teammates who desired a reunion. Garnett was inducted into the Naismith Memorial Basketball Hall of Fame in 2021.

Former Celtics player Ray Allen (right) embraces Kevin Garnett during Garnett's number-retirement ceremony following the game between the Boston Celtics and the Dallas Mavericks at TD Garden on March 13, 2022.
COURTESY OF GETTY IMAGES

Russell, Heinsohn Inducted into Hall of Fame as Coaches

Inductee Tom Heinsohn speaks during the Basketball Hall of Fame Enshrinement Ceremony on September 11, 2015 at the Naismith Basketball Hall of Fame in Springfield, Massachusetts.
COURTESY OF GETTY IMAGES

THE NAISMITH MEMORIAL Basketball Hall of Fame enshrines candidates in several categories, but only a select few are inducted in more than one. Bill Russell and Tom Heinsohn would be considered a select few. Both were inducted as players because of their accomplishments and championships. But both were also enshrined as coaches for their impact on the game after they retired as players. Heinsohn was inducted as a coach in 2015, having led the Celtics to championships in 1974 and 1976, the first titles in the post-Russell era. Heinsohn led the 1970s Big Three of Jo Jo White, Dave Cowens, and John Havlicek to great success after some difficult times in the early 1970s. Russell was inducted as a coach in 2021, having become the first Black coach in NBA history and also having lead the Celtics to titles in 1968 and 1969 as player-coach. Russell also directed the Seattle SuperSonics in the 1970s and Sacramento Kings in the late 1980s before retiring from coaching. Both men were impactful and instrumental as coaches and were given the highest honor. Russell's speech (given from his home in Seattle because of the pandemic) was heartfelt, as he said he was actually humbled by the honor. Heinsohn delivered funny stories during his induction speech about his relationships with his players, team president Red Auerbach, and of course game officials.

Stevens Steps Down as Coach, Replaces Ainge as President

THE 2020–21 CELTICS were tabbed as championship contenders when the season began after reaching the Eastern Conference Finals the previous season. But the club could never get untracked, blowing big leads, being beset by COVID-19 issues, and giving inconsistent performances. Boston finished the season 36–36 and was eliminated by the Brooklyn Nets in the first round. As a coach, Brad Stevens felt like his message to his players wasn't resonating, while president of basketball operations Danny Ainge was ready for a change. So a day after the season ended, Stevens was promoted to president of basketball operations while Ainge stepped down from his post, eventually joining the front office of the Utah Jazz. Stevens wanted more influence in personnel decisions and more impact on how the roster was built, while Ainge's run as a general manager had been a glorious one. Stevens' first move as president was to trade Kemba Walker to the Oklahoma City Thunder for former Celtic Al Horford, a trade that was considered a major success considering Horford's impact on the squad the next season. Stevens also hired former Brooklyn Nets assistant Ime Udoka as head coach, and Udoka led the Celtics to the NBA Finals in his first season. For Stevens, he helped Boston to three Eastern Conference Finals appearances and seven playoff appearances in his eight seasons. Stevens finished fourth all-time in Celtics coaching victories behind Red Auerbach, Tom Heinsohn, and Doc Rivers. Ainge built a championship roster in 2008, built another NBA Finals roster in 2010, and made the pivotal trade of Paul Pierce and Kevin Garnett that netted the draft picks to select Jaylen Brown and Jayson Tatum.

New Celtics coach Brad Stevens (left), confers with Danny Ainge, president of basketball operations for the Celtics, during a Southwest Airlines Orlando Pro Summer League game on July 7, 2013 at Amway Center in Orlando, Florida.
COURTESY OF GETTY IMAGES

Marcus Smart Wins 2022 Defensive Player of the Year Award

FOR SEVEN SEASONS, Marcus Smart feverishly worked to turn himself into a premium NBA defender. He was the sixth overall draft pick by the Celtics in 2014 and became an indispensable part of the team with his leadership, hustle, and ability to make big plays. And although he had been voted first-team All-Defensive for consecutive seasons, Smart never felt truly appreciated until, following the 2021–22 season, he became the first Celtic to win the Defensive Player of the Year award since Kevin Garnett in 2008. Smart was presented with the award after a Celtics practice by ex-Celtic and former Defensive Player of the Year Gary Payton, the last guard to earn the honor in 1996. Smart was grateful about winning his first major award, but it was well deserved. He led the resurrection of the Celtics defense during the 2021–22 season, when Boston was the best in several statistical categories. Smart, with his size and defensive prowess, had the ability to check all five positions, including center. He was used as a multi-positional player during his nine-year Celtics career and was never afraid of big moments. Still, he had always felt underappreciated for his efforts. Smart received 37 first-place votes and 257 total points, edging Phoenix's Mikal Bridges. "I'm a defender, and that's what I do," Smart told reporters "I defend and try to come and be one of the best ones to do it. With this award, all that does is just continues to help me and show me that there's still more to go and to continue the path that I'm on." Smart is also the two-time winner of the NBA's hustle award and a three-time first-team All-Defensive selection.

Marcus Smart #36 defends against Giannis Antetokounmpo #34 of the Milwaukee Bucks during Game 4 of the NBA Playoffs Eastern Conference Semifinals on May 9, 2022 at the Fiserv Forum in Milwaukee, Wisconsin.
COURTESY OF GETTY IMAGES

Bob Cousy waves to the crowd during the NBA at 50, 50th Anniversary All-Time Team ceremony during the NBA All-Star Weekend at the Gund Arena on February 9, 1997 in Cleveland, Ohio. COURTESY OF GETTY IMAGES

Bird, Cousy, Parish, Russell, Walton, McHale Named to the All-Time 50th and 75th Anniversary Teams

THERE WAS NOT much suspense when the NBA named their all-time 50th and 75th anniversary teams about which former Celtics would be chosen. On All-Star Weekend in February 1997, several former Celtics were named to the team and attended the induction ceremony in Cleveland. Larry Bird, Bill Russell, Bob Cousy, Kevin McHale, Bill Walton, Robert Parish, Bill Sharman, and Sam Jones were named to the 50th anniversary team. All but three members (Jerry West, Pete Maravich, and Shaquille O'Neal) of the 50th-anniversary team were present in Cleveland, making the weekend a once-in-a-lifetime experience, with Russell and Wilt Chamberlain reminiscing along with Magic Johnson and Larry Bird. All of the aforementioned players were also named to the 75th anniversary team at All-Star Weekend in Cleveland in 2022. Russell received the honor a few months before his death and was photographed wearing the commemorative jacket in his Seattle-area home. Cousy, then 94, also acknowledged the award on a video presentation during halftime of the All-Star Game. Several newer members of the 75th anniversary team, such as Kevin Garnett and Paul Pierce, were able to catch up with past Celtics and also current All-Stars such as Jayson Tatum.

Eking Out Game 7 of the 2022 Eastern Conference Finals

Boston Celtics hoist the championship trophy after they defeated the Miami Heat 100–96 in game 7 of the NBA Eastern Conference Finals at FTX Arena in Miami, Florida, on May 29, 2022.
COURTESY OF GETTY IMAGES

THE CELTICS TOOK the final two games of their thrilling Eastern Conference semifinal series against the Milwaukee Bucks to advance to the Conference Finals, facing a familiar opponent in the Miami Heat. That series was an emotional tug-of-war, with each team winning on the other's floor. Boston took Game 2 in Miami. The Heat won Game 3 in Boston despite Jaylen Brown's 40 points, and the Celtics responded with two consecutive wins to take control. Jimmy Butler was brilliant in Game 6, scoring 47 points at TD Garden in a Miami win and then guaranteeing that the Heat would win the series. He spoke too soon. With a chance to reach their first NBA Finals in 12 years, the Celtics dominated the first three-and-a-half quarters at FTX Arena and then took a 98–85 lead with three minutes and 35 seconds left. The game appeared decided after Marcus Smart's two free throws, but the Celtics began turning the ball over and allowing easy baskets. Max Strus cut the deficit to two points with a 3-pointer with 50 seconds left. After Smart missed a layup, the Heat raced the ball down the floor with a chance to take the lead, but Butler's pull-up 3-pointer fell short and Al Horford gathered the rebound, securing the Celtics' trip back to the championship series. Jayson Tatum was named MVP of the series, winning the first Larry Bird Award, and there was a collective sigh of relief—because the Celtics did not make things easy on themselves.

Losing to the Warriors: The Agony of Defeat

THE 2022 NBA Finals matchup against the Golden State Warriors began so promisingly, with the Celtics cruising to a Game 1 victory behind brilliant performances from Al Horford and Derrick White and then taking control of the series with a Game 3 win at TD Garden. But the Warriors were championship tested with Stephen Curry, Klay Thompson, and Draymond Green, getting those last two wins would not be easy. Still, Boston punched first in Game 4, looking to take a commanding three-games-to-one lead behind a 16-point first half from Jayson Tatum for a 5-point lead. But Curry responded with a legendary performance in the second half, scoring 24 points as the Warriors overcame a 4-point deficit with five minutes and 18 seconds left to take Game 4. The Celtics lacked experience in those clutch situations. Tatum struggled to score against the defense of Andrew Wiggins, and his teammates couldn't pick up the slack against a Golden State team that sensed vulnerability. The Celtics wouldn't win another Game in the series, losing Game 5 in San Francisco despite a spirited first-half performance and then Game 6 at home after jumping out to a 14–2 lead. The Warriors were the first team to celebrate a title in Boston since the 1985 Lakers, and it was a painful defeat for a rising young team. Tatum, Jaylen Brown, and Smart all promised to use this as a learning experience and make another championship run the next season. Team president of basketball operations Brad Stevens would add to the roster to ensure the Celtics were deeper and more versatile in the future.

Golden State Warriors' Stephen Curry, #30, goes up for a layup against Jaylen Brown, #7, and Robert Williams III, #44, during Game 6 of the NBA Finals at TD Garden on Thursday, June 16, 2022.
COURTESY OF GETTY IMAGES

The Passing of an Icon, Bill Russell

IT SEEMED BILL Russell was invincible, as if he would live forever. After his retirement as a player and coach he remained visible in NBA circles, attending games, receiving much-deserved awards, getting to know today's contemporary players, and joking with some of his old teammates and adversaries with his legendary cackle. He was an icon, the model of the social activist athlete who would not be silenced by his critics or those who believed he should just be quiet and play ball. Even after the Celtics lost the NBA Finals to the Golden State Warriors in June 2022, Russell posted a video promising the Celtics would return in 2023 and win the title this time. So it came as a shock when Russell passed away at age 88 on July 31, 2022. It was a devastating loss for the NBA community, which revered Russell and showered him with the appreciation and kudos he felt he did not receive during his playing career. Tributes poured in for Russell, from the White House to athletes from other sports to current NBA players who had a chance to shake Russell's hand, share a laugh, or listen to countless stories of his experiences. The Celtics and the city of Boston honored Russell over the years despite the all-time great feeling disregarded and disrespected at times during his career. A statue of Russell was erected near City Hall in 2013 and Celtics fans would respond with standing ovations each time he attended games and sit courtside. The NBA responded to Russell's passing by retiring his No. 6 league-wide, similar to Major League Baseball's tribute to Jackie Robinson by retiring number 42. Every NBA arena would have No. 6 painted courtside in front of the scorer's table for the 2022–23 season while the Celtics would place No. 6 on the key on both sides of the floor at TD Garden. The NBA and the Celtics could never repay Russell for his contributions to the game and to society, but they showed their appreciation and reverence during the past few decades with the league naming the NBA Finals MVP award after Russell.

Bill Russell poses for a photo in 1996.
COURTESY OF GETTY IMAGES

The Joe Mazzulla Era Begins

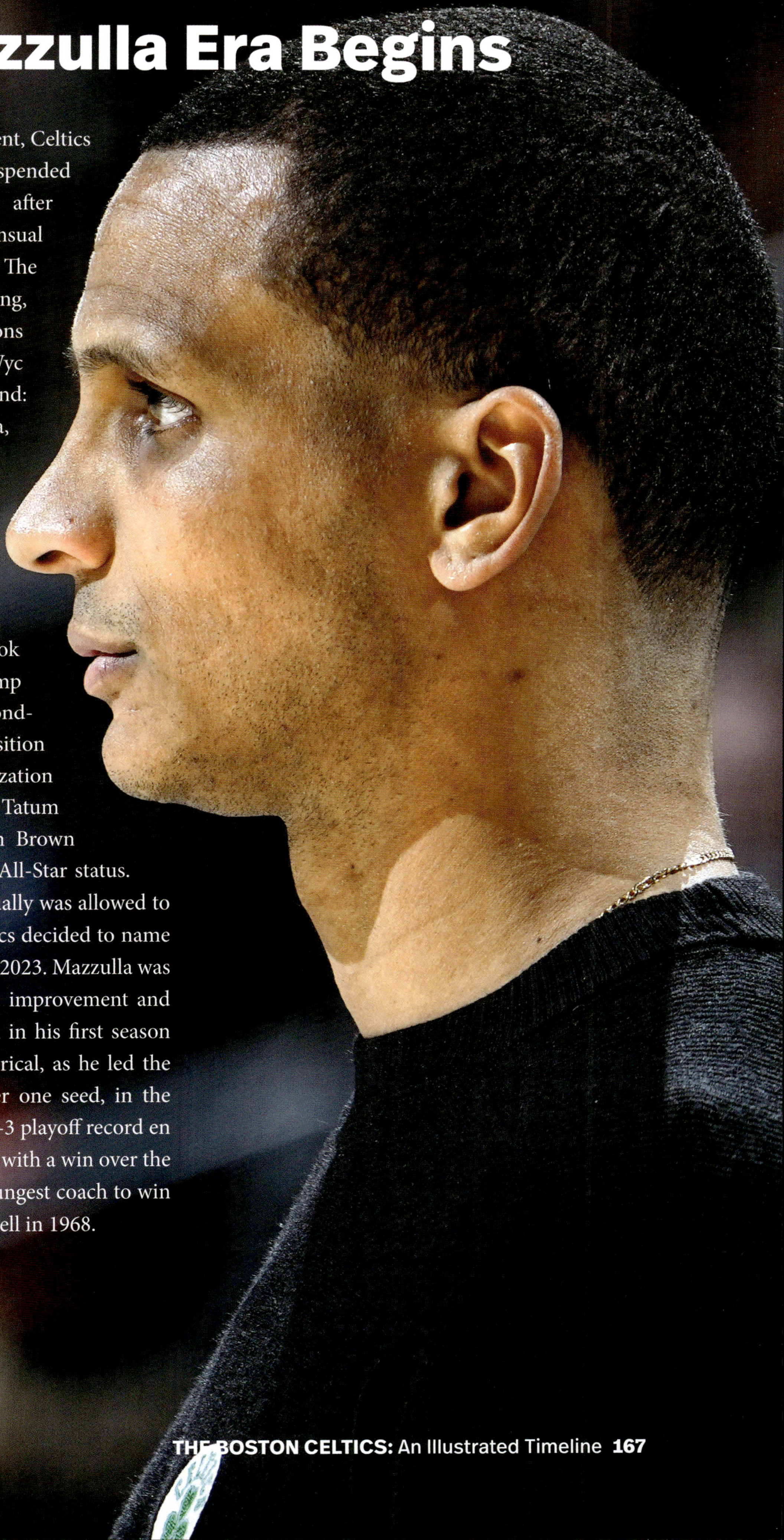

IN A SHOCKING development, Celtics coach Ime Udoka was suspended for the 2022–23 season after inappropriate actions in a consensual relationship with a Celtics employee. The situation left the organization reeling, but president of basketball operations Brad Stevens and majority governor Wyc Grousbeck had a replacement in mind: assistant coach Joe Mazzulla. Mazzulla, 34, had been a Celtics assistant since 2019 when he joined Stevens's staff, and he became popular with the players because of his work ethic and professionalism. He was the perfect choice to lead a team with championship aspirations. Mazzulla took over at the beginning of training camp and led the Celtics to the NBA's second-best record in 2022–23. The transition transpired as smoothly as the organization could have expected, with Jayson Tatum playing at an MVP level while Jaylen Brown taking the next step toward perennial All-Star status. Udoka remained suspended and eventually was allowed to pursue other coaching jobs as the Celtics decided to name Mazzulla permanent coach in February 2023. Mazzulla was the driving force behind the defensive improvement and had taken the Celtics to the next level in his first season as coach. His second season was historical, as he led the Celtics to a 64–18 record, the number one seed, in the Eastern Conference and a sparkling 16–3 playoff record en route to the Celtics' 18th championship with a win over the Dallas Mavericks. At 35, he was the youngest coach to win an NBA title since 34-year-old Bill Russell in 1968.

Head Coach Joe Mazzulla looks on from the sideline during a game against the Denver Nuggets on January 1, 2023 at the Ball Arena in Denver, Colorado.
COURTESY OF GETTY IMAGES

Tatum and Brown Reach Unprecedented Heights

THE FUTURE OF the Boston Celtics is secure, thanks to the presence of two elite superstars in Jayson Tatum and Jaylen Brown. They were drafted third overall, a year apart, and were tabbed as potential cornerstones. Both were thrown immediately into the fire as the Celtics were contenders and chasing that elusive 18th championship. They immediately teamed to help Boston get to the Eastern Conference Finals in 2018, with Tatum stunning fans with his dunk on LeBron James in Game 7. And since that run, the Jays have been forever linked but their journey hasn't always been easy. After playoff failures, there was concern as to whether they could co-exist because their games were too similar. There were questions as to whether they actually were friends. There were pundits who believed the Celtics' best route would be to separate the two and trade Brown. Those concerns were squelched as the Celtics continued their deep playoff runs. The dynamic duo of Brown and Tatum helped Boston finally overcome its main nemesis in the Miami Heat and reach the NBA Finals in 2022. Although the Celtics lost that series in six games to the Golden State Warriors, it served as a learning experience and motivation for the two. And as their games expanded on the court, their friendship and regard for each other grew off the floor. They needed each other. And the Celtics needed them. After another disheartening playoff elimination in 2023, the Jays were determined to reach the top of the NBA mountain. They both sacrificed their games as president of basketball operations Brad Stevens added more talent, and they displayed their versatility and prowess most when it counted. They led Boston on a stellar playoff run in 2024, all the way with to the franchise's 18th championship. They celebrated. They embraced each other and embraced being part of franchise history and placed on the list of all-time Celtics greats.

Jaylen Brown #7 and Jayson Tatum look on during Game 4 of the NBA Playoffs Eastern Conference Finals on May 23, 2022 at TD Garden.
COURTESY OF GETTY IMAGES

Celtics Trade for Porzingis, Holiday, Say Goodbye to Marcus Smart

THE CELTICS WERE devastated by their loss to the Miami Heat in the Eastern Conference Finals, and president of basketball operations Brad Stevens sought opportunities to adjust and upgrade the roster. The decisions were difficult but necessary. In June 2023, he made a controversial deal, sending senior member Marcus Smart, his first draft pick as coach, to the Memphis Grizzlies for versatile center Kristaps Porzingis. A few months later, Stevens moved popular center Robert Williams and Sixth Man of the Year Malcolm Brogdon to the Portland Trail Blazers for Jrue Holiday, the former All-Star, NBA champion, and Olympian who helped galvanize the franchise in his first season. Stevens has never been afraid to make bold moves, but trading the popular Smart, considered the heart and soul of the team, was a gut-wrenching but necessary move that eventually paid off with the franchise's 18th championship. Holiday was named All-Defensive Second Team in his first season and then signed a lucrative contract extension to remain in Boston long term.

Kristaps Porzingis smiles during a game against the Brooklyn Nets during the In-Season Tournament on November 10, 2023 at TD Garden in Boston.
COURTESY OF GETTY IMAGES

Jaylen Brown Signs Contract Extension

FOR YEARS, OBSERVERS wondered whether Jaylen Brown could co-exist with Jayson Tatum, whether he liked Boston, and whether he would be a long-term cornerstone. In July 2023, the Celtics demonstrated just how dedicated they were to keeping their former third overall pick long term by signing Brown to a five-year, $304 million deal, making him in the highest paid player in the NBA. During his press conference, which was held during one of his various community service efforts, Brown said he wanted to use his new contract and his commitment to Boston to help even the wealth disparity between the white communities and disadvantaged communities in the city of Boston. Brown is a three-time All-Star, was a second-team All-NBA selection in 2023 and quieted his critics by winning the Eastern Conference Finals MVP and NBA Finals MVP in leading the Celtics to their 18th title. The new contract was well worth it for the franchise.

Jaylen Brown (center) looks at president of basketball operations Brad Stevens after signing his supermax contract extension. Standing behind them are (from left) Celtics governor Wyc Grousbeck, managing general partner Steve Pagliuca, and head coach Joe Mazzulla.
COURTESY OF GETTY IMAGES

Jayson Tatum Meets Larry Bird

FOR MANY OF the current Celtics, Larry Bird has only been a superstar on a grainy YouTube video. Bird, the Celtics' all-time great forward, three-time NBA champion, and three-time MVP, has kept a lower profile in the past several years and had not made many trips to Boston. But something special happened at All-Star Weekend in Indianapolis in February 2024. Before he was going out to warm up for the Eastern Conference Team, current Celtics superstar Jayson Tatum saw Bird sitting on the bench, and the two Boston icons, one past, one present, met for the first time. The two chatted briefly, and Tatum asked an NBA photographer to take a photo. Tatum said it was an honor to meet Bird and that the all-time great was taller than he expected. Bird expressed his admiration for Tatum and wished him the best. It made Tatum's All-Star Weekend.

Jayson Tatum is introduced before the NBA All-Star Game as part of All-Star Weekend on Sunday, February 18, 2024 at Gainbridge Fieldhouse in Indianapolis, Indiana.
COURTESY OF GETTY IMAGES

Celtics Clinch Best Record in NBA

THE CELTICS ENTERED the 2023–24 season with a retooled roster that included Kristaps Porzingis, Jrue Holiday, and an improved Derrick White. After the disappointing end to the 2022–23 season, the Celtics began this season on a mission, winning 20 of their first 25 games and 48 of their first 60. Boston seized the top seed in the Eastern Conference and held on to that spot for the entire season, never losing more than two consecutive games and finishing fifth all time in point differential, beating opponents by an average of 11.34 points per game. Jayson Tatum and Jaylen Brown were named to the All-Star Team while Derrick White and Jrue Holiday were named All-Defensive Second Team. The 64 wins were the fourth most in the illustrious team history and the most since the 2007–08 team (which won the NBA Championship) won 66 games.

Jaylen Brown #7, and Jayson Tatum embrace during the game against the Atlanta Hawks on March 28, 2024, at the State Farm Arena in Atlanta, Georgia.
COURTESY OF GETTY IMAGES

Jaylen Brown (holding trophy) celebrates after winning the Eastern Conference Finals MVP after Game 4 against the Indiana Pacers on May 27, 2024, at Gainbridge Fieldhouse in Indianapolis, Indiana.
COURTESY OF GETTY IMAGES

Celtics Advance to Second Finals in Three Years

BOSTON'S QUEST for title 18 continued with an impressive playoff run, as the Celtics went 12–2 in the first three rounds, including a sweep of the Indiana Pacers in the Eastern Conference Finals to advance to their second Finals series in three years. The Celtics went 6–0 on the road during their run through the East and won a handful of clutch games, including the final two against the Pacers. Jaylen Brown made key plays during the Indiana series, including a 3-pointer to send Game 1 into overtime and then a 40-point performance in Game 2 to help the Celtics secure the series win. A team that had been criticized in recent years for lackadaisical play in key stretches and blowing games to extend series took care of business in the East. Boston used players such as Jayson Tatum, Derrick White, and Jrue Holiday to win the final three games of series against Miami and Cleveland and swept Indiana to return to the apex of NBA basketball.

Finally, Title No. 18

IT WAS the final hurdle of a 10-year journey for the Boston Celtics. After knocking on the door of a championship repeatedly in the past several years, the Celtics were not going to be denied this time, topping the Dallas Mavericks in five games to win their 18th NBA championship and first in 16 years. Jaylen Brown, the former third overall pick whose draft selection had been jeered by some Celtics fans eight years earlier, earned the NBA Finals MVP award with a stellar defensive series, taking on the assignment of guarding superstar Luka Doncic. Jayson Tatum led the Celtics in points, rebounds, and assists during the postseason and expressed relief and delight after winning his first championship. Tatum and Brown had accomplished everything besides a championship, playing in 107 postseason games together before winning their first crown. Coach Joe Mazzulla became the second-youngest Celtics coach to win a championship at age 35, in only his second season as coach. It completed one of the most dominant seasons in Celtics history as Boston finished the postseason with a sparkling 16–3 record.

(From left to right) Jayson Tatum, Jaylen Brown, and Jaden Springer pose with the Larry O'Brien and Bill Russell Finals MVP Trophys after Game 5 against the Dallas Mavericks of the NBA Finals on June 17, 2024 at TD Garden.
COURTESY OF GETTY IMAGES

ALL IMAGES COURTESY OF GETTY IMAGES

Sources

ESPN.com
Basketball-Reference.com
https://www.basketball-reference.com/teams/BOS/
Celtics.com
YouTube.com
https://www.youtube.com/watch?v=J4fTjcJwlmw
https://www.youtube.com/watch?v=3CTJ7xPrhfQ&t=4338s
https://www.youtube.com/watch?v=Xla5JjkA43Q
https://www.youtube.com/watch?v=o_cyvav5tvk
https://www.youtube.com/watch?v=waDLzWgge7I
https://www.youtube.com/watch?v=Lnu5vMfPtbw&t=207s
https://www.youtube.com/watch?v=n3WMg_5SESo
https://www.youtube.com/watch?v=OEMbEanJdXc
https://www.youtube.com/watch?v=XyP_BPb1mEw
https://www.youtube.com/watch?v=aXFoF2dEZJc
https://www.youtube.com/watch?v=KUd4PG8EyQ8
BostonGlobe.com/Sports
Landofbasketball.com
WashingtonPost.com
NBA.com
SportsIllustrated.com

Index

Index

Index